Excel
Get the Results You Want!

Year 4
Thinking Skills
Tests

**Sharon Dalgleish,
Tanya Dalgleish
& Hamish McLean**

PASCAL
PRESS

Completely new edition incorporating 2021 Opportunity Class Test changes

ISBN 978 174125 701 4

Pascal Press Pty Ltd
PO Box 250
Glebe NSW 2037
(02) 8585 4050
www.pascalpress.com.au

Publisher: Vivienne Joannou
Project editor: Mark Dixon
Edited by Mark Dixon and Rosemary Peers
Proofread by Mark Dixon
Answers checked by Dale Little and Peter Little
Cover by DiZign Pty Ltd
Typeset by Grizzly Graphics (Leanne Richters)
Printed by Vivar Printing/Green Giant Press

Notice of liability
The information contained in this book is distributed without warranty. While precautions have been taken in the preparation of this material, neither the authors nor Pascal Press shall have any liability to any person or entity with respect to any liability, loss or damage caused or alleged to be caused directly or indirectly by the instructions and content contained in the book.

Contents

Test skill explanation and practice pages

Sample tests

Answers

ABOUT THIS BOOK

This book has been written to help develop students' thinking skills. Thinking skills involve two disciplines: critical thinking and problem solving.

Critical thinking means the ability to analyse a claim or argument; identify whether it is flawed or uses correct reasoning; and determine whether the evidence, assumptions and conclusion are warranted.

Problem solving as a thinking skill means the ability to use numerical or mathematical skills to work out solutions to problems. These include visualising and rotating solids in three-dimensional space; ordering a number of objects based on comparisons and characteristics; analysing graphs and diagrams; and solving mathematical puzzles involving numbers, shapes and time.

Critical-thinking and problem-solving skills are valuable in everyday life as well as in many fields of endeavour students might eventually embark upon.

The first section of this book teaches students 18 thinking skills. Each thinking skill is first defined, then a sample question is provided and the solution is worked through for the student as a teaching/learning exercise. Then two practice questions are provided. These are for the student to attempt independently. The solutions are worked through in the answer section of the book.

This section is followed by ten practice tests comprising 15 questions each. Each test includes an equal mixture of critical-thinking and problem-solving questions.

Answers and detailed explanations are provided at the back of the book. Most answers include the working out.

If you would like to use this book to help you prepare specifically for the Opportunity Class Test, you can merge two Sample Tests and have your child complete the two tests in 30 minutes.

One test will therefore comprise 30 questions, which is equivalent to the length of the Thinking Skills paper in the NSW Opportunity Class Placement Test. For example, you could merge Sample Test 1A with Sample Test 1B to form Test 1.

ABOUT THE OPPORTUNITY CLASS TEST

This book is excellent preparation for the Thinking Skills section of the NSW Opportunity Class Placement Test, which is taken by students in Year 4.

The NSW Opportunity Class Placement Test is required for placement in an Opportunity Class in a NSW public school.

This type of class offers an extra challenge for academically gifted students with high potential in Years 5 and 6. Selection is based on academic merit.

Details are available at: https://education.nsw.gov.au/public-schools/selective-high-schools-and-opportunity-classes/year-5.

INTRODUCTION

The NSW Opportunity Class Placement Test consists of three multiple-choice tests:

- **Reading** (25 questions in 30 minutes)
- **Mathematical Reasoning** (35 questions in 40 minutes)
- **Thinking Skills** (30 questions in 30 minutes).

ADVICE TO STUDENTS

Each question in the NSW Opportunity Class Placement Test is multiple choice. This means you have to choose the correct answer from the given options. You need to read the question in the test booklet then mark your answer on a separate answer sheet.

We have included a sample answer sheet in this book—similar to those you will be given in the actual test—for you to practise on.

Under time pressure and test conditions it is possible to miss a question and leave a line on the answer sheet blank. Always check that your answer on the separate answer sheet is written down next to the right number. For instance, check that your answer to question 15 is written down against the number 15 on the answer sheet. There is nothing worse than finding out you have missed a space, especially when time is running short.

Some of the more challenging Thinking Skills problem-solving questions, for example, could take you up to 10 minutes to complete to begin with, as you may use diagrams or tables to help you solve them. Remember that the more questions you do of this same type, the faster you will become—until you know exactly how to solve them.

Thinking Skills—Sample Answer Sheet

Mark your answers here.

To answer each question, fill in the appropriate circle for your chosen answer.

Use a pencil. If you make a mistake or change your mind, erase and try again.

You can make extra copies of this answer sheet to mark your answers to all the Sample Tests in this book.

Test A

1 A B C D ○○○○	6 A B C D ○○○○	11 A B C D ○○○○
2 A B C D ○○○○	7 A B C D ○○○○	12 A B C D ○○○○
3 A B C D ○○○○	8 A B C D ○○○○	13 A B C D ○○○○
4 A B C D ○○○○	9 A B C D ○○○○	14 A B C D ○○○○
5 A B C D ○○○○	10 A B C D ○○○○	15 A B C D ○○○○

Test B

1 A B C D ○○○○	6 A B C D ○○○○	11 A B C D ○○○○
2 A B C D ○○○○	7 A B C D ○○○○	12 A B C D ○○○○
3 A B C D ○○○○	8 A B C D ○○○○	13 A B C D ○○○○
4 A B C D ○○○○	9 A B C D ○○○○	14 A B C D ○○○○
5 A B C D ○○○○	10 A B C D ○○○○	15 A B C D ○○○○

Identifying the main idea

- The main idea is the idea or conclusion the creator of the text wants you to accept is true. It's often stated at the beginning of a text but could also be at the end or anywhere else in the text. The rest of the text will support or add to, or give you reasons to believe, this main idea.

- Read the question text carefully and think about what the creator of the text wants you to accept. Underline the sentence you think could be the main idea. Check to see if the rest of the text gives you reasons to believe this main idea. Read each answer option in turn to evaluate if it expresses the main idea. Quickly eliminate any answers that are definitely wrong.

SAMPLE QUESTION

Mathematicians should love eating Romanesco broccoli. It is yellow-green in colour and looks a bit like a cauliflower. However, it displays two amazing mathematical qualities: fractals and Fibonacci sequence. Fractals appear the same at different scales. The spiral form of a Romanesco is a fractal structure. Each bud is made up of a series of smaller buds. Each smaller bud is a copy of the larger bud. In a Fibonacci sequence the next number is found by adding together the two previous numbers. And that's exactly the sequence of the number of spirals on the head of a Romanesco!

Which statement best expresses the main idea of the text?

A Romanesco looks like cauliflower.

B Romanesco displays two mathematical qualities.

C Romanesco is rich in vitamin C.

D Mathematicians love eating Romanesco.

B is correct. The main idea the creator of the text wants you to accept is that Romanesco displays two amazing mathematical qualities. The rest of the text gives more information about fractals and Fibonacci sequence to support this main idea.

A is incorrect. This background information is used in the introduction but is not the main idea.

C is incorrect. This information is not in the text so cannot be the main idea.

D is incorrect. The introduction states that mathematicians **should** love eating this vegetable, not that they love it. So D cannot be the main idea.

Practice questions

1 Moira Newi was the first Indigenous woman to receive a medal for heroic conduct. In 1899 a tropical cyclone in Far North Queensland wiped out a fleet of pearling boats. Hundreds of sailors and pearlers drowned. Moira, a 15 year old from the Torres Strait Islands, was a pearler on one of the boats that sank. She bravely battled the raging seas for seven hours, swimming more than three kilometres through the storm. What's more, she did this with her two older sisters clinging to her back!

Which statement best expresses the main idea of the text?

A Moira Newi swam with her sisters on her back.

B Hundreds of sailors and pearlers drowned in a tropical cyclone in 1899.

C Moira Newi received a medal for heroic conduct.

D A pearler is a person who dives for pearls.

2 The 100 Year Starship is a project created to research and plan for humans to travel to other stars. It brings together experts from the areas of space, life sciences and technology. The team began work in 2012, using research and imagination to develop new ideas. The aim is that humans will be able to build a real starship by 2112.

Which statement best expresses the main idea of the text?

A The 100 Year Starship team uses research and imagination to develop ideas.

B It takes 100 years to build a starship.

C The 100 Year Starship project brings together many different experts.

D The aim of the 100 Year Starship project is for humans to travel to other stars.

Identifying a conclusion that must be true

- To draw a conclusion you need to read and assess all the information and evidence provided. A conclusion can only be true if it is supported by evidence. A conclusion can be eliminated if there is evidence that contradicts it, or if there is no evidence or incomplete evidence to support it.
- Read the question carefully. Judge which conclusion must be true based on the evidence in the text. As you read the answer options, try to quickly eliminate any conclusion that has evidence to contradict it. Also eliminate any conclusion that is neither proved nor disproved because the evidence is incomplete or unavailable.

SAMPLE QUESTION

> Faisal was heading to the pet store to buy his dog some new toys.

Faisal: 'I'd like a new ball for the park. But if I can't get a ball, then I'll buy a tug toy. And if I do get a ball, then I'll also buy a new fluffy toy instead of a chew toy.'

If Faisal doesn't buy a tug toy, what does he buy at the pet store?

A a ball and a fluffy toy

B a fluffy toy and a chew toy

C a ball only

D a chew toy only

A is correct. If Faisal doesn't buy a tug toy, then you can conclude he buys a new ball for the park. And since he buys a ball, then he will also buy a fluffy toy.
B is incorrect. Faisal says he will buy a fluffy toy or a chew toy, not both.
C is incorrect. Faisal says that if he buys a ball, he will also buy a new fluffy toy.
D is incorrect. If Faisal buys a chew toy, you can conclude he will also buy a tug toy.

Practice questions

1. When Bree was applying to attend an advanced filmmaking workshop, one of the instructors told her: 'To have even a chance of being accepted into the workshop you must have already made at least five films.'

   If Bree's instructor is correct, which one of these statements will be true?
   A All of the applicants who have already made five films will be accepted into the workshop.
   B Only the applicants who have made less than five films will be accepted into the workshop.
   C None of the applicants who have made less than five films will be accepted into the workshop.
   D Some of the applicants who have made less than five films will be accepted into the workshop.

2. Emma, Hank and Ilya are planning a trip to the zoo. They are trying to decide what animals they will see, since there is not enough time to see all the animals. Emma says she wants to see the vultures, condors, snakes, meerkats and wombats. Hank says he wants to see the giraffes, wombats and meerkats. Ilya says he wants to see the condors, crocodiles, meerkats, platypuses and wombats.

   Which animals does Emma want to see that neither Hank nor Ilya wants to?
   A condors and vultures
   B vultures and snakes
   C snakes and meerkats
   D platypuses and giraffes

Identifying a conclusion that is not possible

- To be able to draw a conclusion you need to consider all the evidence. For a conclusion to be true or correct it has to be supported by evidence. You can work out when a conclusion is not possible or cannot be true because there won't be evidence to support it.
- Read the question carefully. When working out your answer you should try to quickly eliminate any options that are obviously incorrect. These will be the conclusions that are true. This will narrow down your choice.
- Judge which conclusion cannot be true by deciding that there is no evidence to support it.

SAMPLE QUESTION

The wildlife park opens Tuesday to Sunday from 10 am to 5 pm with extended hours 9 am to 6 pm during school holidays. Rita and Tom visited during the summer months.

If the above information is true, only one of the sentences below **cannot** be true. Which one?

A Rita and Tom entered the wildlife park at 11 am on Wednesday 10 January.

B Rita and Tom visited the park between midday and 4 pm on Thursday 15 December.

C Rita and Tom stayed until 6 pm on Monday 10 January.

D Rita and Tom visited until 6 pm on a Sunday afternoon in February.

C is correct. This conclusion cannot be true because the wildlife park is not open on Mondays.
A is incorrect because it could be true. The park opens at 10 am on a Wednesday.
B is incorrect because it could be true. The park opens from 10 am to 5 pm on Thursdays in May.
D is incorrect because it could be true. The park is open until 6 pm on Sunday afternoons in summer. February is a summer month so the wildlife park has extended opening hours.

Practice questions

1 Ashlee wants a new fridge. There is an offer available that if you buy a fridge, you get a portable cooler for free. Another store is offering $100 of groceries with every fridge purchased. The fridge Ashlee wants is the same price at each store but delivery costs $50 from each store. A third store is offering free delivery and the fridge is the same price but there's no free gift.

If the above information is true, only one of the sentences below **cannot** be true. Which one?

A Ashlee purchased a fridge and got $100 worth of groceries with free delivery.

B Ashlee decided not to buy a new fridge after all.

C Ashlee purchased a fridge and got it delivered for free but did not get a portable cooler.

D Ashlee purchased a fridge and had it delivered for free.

2 The violin teacher told Henry that to have any chance of improving his violin-playing skills he must practise at least twice a week for an hour each time. Henry currently practises every Wednesday for two hours but is tired after the first hour so doesn't improve at all during the second hour of practice.

If the above information is correct, which one of the following is **not** possible?

A Henry continues practising only on Wednesdays for two hours and doesn't improve his playing.

B Henry continues practising only on Wednesdays for two hours and improves his playing.

C Henry decides to only practise for one hour on a Wednesday and doesn't improve his playing.

D Henry gives up playing the violin because he doesn't have the time or the inclination to continue practising.

Identifying evidence that leads to a conclusion

- To draw a conclusion you need data or evidence that supports the conclusion. Sometimes you can't work out a conclusion because there isn't enough evidence.
- These types of questions ask you to identify which information allows you to know a conclusion. These questions are not asking you to draw a conclusion but instead to judge which option helps you to know the conclusion. You need to eliminate the options that won't lead to a conclusion or that don't help you work out a conclusion.

SAMPLE QUESTION

Polly has asked for a microscope, a pair of binoculars and a skateboard for her birthday. Five family members decided to put in some of the money each to buy one of the items for Polly's birthday. Her aunt wanted to buy her a microscope. Her uncle and cousin said they should buy the binoculars. Her grandmother and grandfather both thought a skateboard would be best. The family members could not agree so they decided to have a vote where each one of them had to vote for two of the items. The item that everyone voted for would be the item purchased.

Knowing **one** of the following would allow us to know the result of the vote. Which one is it?

A Each person voted for either the microscope or the binoculars, or both.

B The skateboard was one of the more popular votes.

C Nobody voted for both the skateboard and the microscope.

D Only two people voted for the microscope.

C is correct. All five people had two votes each. Knowing that nobody voted for both the skateboard and the microscope tells you that everyone voted for the binoculars, i.e. they must have voted for the binoculars and the skateboard or the binoculars and the microscope. Knowing this information allows you to work out that the binoculars were purchased.

A is incorrect. Knowing this information is not enough to allow you to work out the conclusion.

B is incorrect. Knowing this information is not enough to allow you to work out the conclusion. It only implies that the skateboard could be the winner.

D is incorrect. Knowing this information is not enough to allow you to work out the conclusion. It only tells you that the microscope did not win the vote.

🖉 Practice questions

1 Jamie made a cake for Harold and his friends in aged care. Jamie had all the ingredients to make a sponge cake, a chocolate cake or a banana cake.

Which **two** statements below most help you to draw a conclusion about which cake Jamie chose to make?

1 Chocolate cake is one of Harold's favourite cakes.
2 One of Harold's friends doesn't particularly like the taste of bananas.
3 Sponge cake is Harold's least favourite cake.
4 One of Harold's best friends is allergic to chocolate.

A 1 and 2   B 1 and 3
C 3 and 4   D 3 and 4

2 Sammi's class was given a choice of theme for the class end-of-year party. They could vote to dress up as monsters, book characters or not to dress up at all. Each student got two votes but they were not allowed to vote for the same option twice. The class will only get to dress up if one of the options is voted for by everyone in the class. Every option got at least one vote.

Knowing **one** of the following would allow us to know the result of the vote. Which one is it?

A Every student voted for either not dressing up at all or for book characters, or both.

B Only two students voted to not dress up at all.

C Monsters was one of the two more popular votes.

D No student voted for both dressing up as a monster and not to dress up at all.

Identifying an assumption

- An assumption is not stated in a text. It is something missing that has been assumed or taken for granted to draw a conclusion. An assumption is not necessarily true but the person making the assumption believes it is. For this reason, making assumptions can lead to incorrect conclusions.
- To identify an assumption in a text, read the text carefully and identify the conclusion that has been made. Next identify the evidence on which this conclusion is based. Finally read and think about each answer option. Which one of these options would you need to take for granted in order to draw this conclusion from the evidence?

SAMPLE QUESTION

All the students at Jade's school were in a special assembly. The headmaster was talking about the school carnival to be held next month. Jade was excited about the carnival. She started talking about it to her friend Eman. The headmaster saw them talking and told them to come to the office after assembly.

Jade: 'There's nothing wrong with talking in assembly. Everyone else does!'

Which assumption has Jade made to draw her conclusion?

A There's nothing wrong with talking in assembly.

B Eman is not going to the carnival.

C Everyone else talks in assembly.

D It's okay to do something if everyone else does it.

D is correct. Jade's conclusion is that there is nothing wrong with talking in assembly. She has based this conclusion on the evidence that everyone else does. So for her conclusion to hold it must be assumed that it is okay to do something if everyone else does it. (Everyone else talks in assembly + it's okay to do something if everyone else does it means therefore there's nothing wrong with talking in assembly.)

A is incorrect. This is Jade's conclusion, not her assumption.

B is incorrect. This assumption does not support Jade's conclusion that there is nothing wrong with talking in assembly.

C is incorrect. This is the evidence Jade has used to base her conclusion on.

 Practice questions

❶ The pet store displayed an advertisement in its window:

Cute kittens for sale!
They'll be gone quickly …
everyone will want one!

Which assumption has the writer of the advertisement made to draw the conclusion in the advertisement?

A The pet store wants to sell the kittens.

B The pet store has cute kittens for sale.

C Everyone likes kittens.

D Everyone will want a kitten.

❷ **Mari:** 'Bruno scored a goal in the soccer match on Saturday.'

Aziz: 'Wow! Bruno is a good soccer player!'

Which assumption has Aziz made to draw his conclusion?

A Anyone who scores a goal is a good soccer player.

B Mari likes soccer.

C Bruno is a good soccer player.

D Bruno scored a goal at soccer on Saturday.

Identifying correct reasoning

- When someone presents a point of view or makes a claim or an argument they use reasoning to support that point of view or argument. Their reasoning must make sense and be based on the facts available.
- When you read or listen to a point of view or argument you need to analyse the reasoning. If the reasoning is correct, you might accept the argument. If the reasoning does not make sense or is flawed, you can reject the claim or argument.
- These kinds of questions ask you to judge if the reasoning is correct. Read the question carefully. When working out your answer quickly eliminate answers that are obviously incorrect until you find the answer that is correct.

SAMPLE QUESTION

Huntsman and tarantula spiders are large and hairy looking. The largest spider in the world by body mass is the Goliath bird-eating tarantula but the Giant huntsman can have a leg span of up to 30 cm so it's sometimes called the largest spider in the world. A huntsman's legs are generally longer than a tarantula's while tarantulas are generally hairier looking than huntsman spiders.

Adele: 'That spider is large and hairy looking so it must be a tarantula.'
Corey: 'But it's got long legs so it must be a huntsman.'

If the information in the box is true, whose reasoning is correct?

A Adele only
B Corey only
C Both Adele and Corey
D Neither Adele nor Corey

D is correct because neither Adele nor Corey are correct in their reasoning.
A is incorrect. Adele wants you to accept her argument that the spider is a tarantula. She gives the reason that it is large and hairy looking. The information in the box tells you that huntsman and tarantula spiders are both large and hairy looking. The fact that the spider seems large and hairy to Adele doesn't mean it must be a tarantula so Adele's reasoning is incorrect. A more reasoned statement would have been that it might be a tarantula because it is big and hairy.
B is incorrect. The fact that Corey thinks the spider has long legs does not mean it must be a huntsman so Corey's reasoning is incorrect. The text in the box tells you that a huntsman's legs are generally longer than a tarantula's. A more reasoned statement would have been that it could be a huntsman because it seems to have very long legs.
C is incorrect. Neither Adele nor Corey uses correct reasoning.

Practice questions

1 Only those students who have completed their workbook pages satisfactorily will be allowed to play indoor games after lunch.

Joshi: 'Martin has not completed his workbook pages so he definitely won't be able to play indoor games after lunch.'

Ella: 'Vivian has completed her workbook pages so she will be allowed to play indoor games after lunch.'

Identifying correct reasoning

If the information in the box is true, whose reasoning is correct?

A Joshi only

B Ella only

C Both Joshi and Ella

D Neither Joshi nor Ella

The petrol icon on the car's dashboard lights up orange when the car is starting to run low on fuel. The petrol light flashes red when there's only enough fuel for ten kilometres of travel.

Caitlin: 'The petrol icon is useful for telling when the tank is full.'

Benedict: 'If the petrol icon is not orange or red, there's no need to refuel urgently.'

Mei: 'If the petrol icon is orange, you've run out of fuel.'

Peter: 'If the petrol light flashes red, you need to find a petrol station within 20 kilometres.'

If the information in the box is true, whose reasoning is correct?

A Caitlin

B Benedict

C Mei

D Peter

Identifying flawed reasoning

- When someone presents a point of view or makes a claim or an argument they use reasoning to support that point of view or argument. Their reasoning must make sense and be based on the facts available.
- When you read or listen to a point of view or argument you need to analyse the reasoning. If the reasoning does not make sense or is flawed, you can reject the claim or argument.
- These kinds of questions ask you to identify if someone has used reasoning that is incorrect or flawed. Read the question carefully. When working out your answer quickly eliminate answers that are obviously incorrect until you find the answer that is correct: the one with flawed reasoning.

SAMPLE QUESTION

Daisy: 'If you hope to make it onto the soccer team as goalkeeper, you need to practise saving goals at least four times a week for half an hour.'
Hannah: 'I practise four times a week for half an hour each time so I'll get the position of goalkeeper.'

If what Daisy says is true, which of the following shows Hannah's mistake?

A A number of players want to be goalkeeper.
B Practice is important but experience playing in games is equally important.
C Practising for the minimum amount of time doesn't guarantee Hannah will get the position.
D Goalkeeper is a challenging position that requires a lot of practice.

C is correct. Daisy has advised that Hannah must practise at least four times a week for half an hour to have any hope of getting the position of goalkeeper on the soccer team. Hannah has incorrectly reasoned that if she does the minimum amount of practice, she'll get the position. The minimum amount of practice might not be enough to make Hannah the best goalkeeper available so Hannah cannot state with certainty that she will get the position of goalkeeper.
A is incorrect. The statement that a number of players want to be goalkeeper might be true but is not the mistake in reasoning made by Hannah.
B and D are incorrect. These statements might be true but they are not the mistake made by Hannah.

 Practice questions

1 Nobody likes a dry cake. Sugar is a commonly used ingredient in cake recipes. It makes a cake moist. It you reduce the amount of sugar in a cake, you risk making the cake dry. Also don't overbake your cake. Overbaking can make it dry too.

Jing baked a cake. The recipe told him to use 1½ cups of sugar and to bake it at 180 degrees for one hour. His cake was dry.

If the information in the box is true, whose reasoning is incorrect?

A **Vanessa**: 'Jing must have left the cake in the oven too long.'
B **Ed**: 'Jing might not have measured exactly 1½ cups of sugar.'
C **Ollie**: 'Maybe Jing used less sugar than the recipe needed.'
D **Amy**: 'It's possible that Jing overbaked the cake in an oven that was too hot.'

2 Polly and Dom are in the supermarket.

Polly: 'Gran asked me to buy her soy milk that comes in a blue-and-white carton. She couldn't remember the brand. There's a lot of different soy milks on the shelves.'

Dom: 'Here's soy milk in a blue-and-white carton. This must be it!'

Which statement below shows the mistake Dom has made?

A Dom doesn't like to drink soy milk.
B Gran might not like the soy milk Dom has found.
C Dom has found Gran's soy milk in the blue-and-white carton.
D There could be more than one brand of soy milk that uses blue and white on the carton.

Identifying additional evidence to strengthen a claim

- When someone makes a claim or presents an argument they use evidence to convince others to accept that claim. A claim can be strengthened with further evidence or additional information.
- To identify the statement that best supports or most strengthens a claim or an argument, read the text carefully. Identify the claim being made in the text. Then consider the answer options listed and assess the impact of each one on that claim. Look for the option that gives further evidence to support the claim or that most strengthens it. Try to quickly eliminate answers which are definitely incorrect or irrelevant to the argument.

SAMPLE QUESTION

Tyler: 'I need to stop at the supermarket on the way home to get some vegetables for dinner tonight. My fridge is empty.'

Zara: 'We could stop at that new farmers' market instead. Vegetables sold at farmers' markets are healthier. They are all locally grown and fresher.'

Which one of these statements, if true, best supports Zara's claim?

A The produce at the market is ripened before harvesting to increase vitamins.

B The supermarket is closed for renovations.

C Most of the vegetables sold at the market were grown using pesticides.

D The farmers' market is close to home.

A is correct. Zara claims that vegetables sold at farmers' markets are healthier than vegetables sold at supermarkets. She supports this by saying that the market vegetables are locally grown and fresher. The statement that the market produce is ripened to increase vitamins is further evidence to support her claim.

B is incorrect. This statement does not support a claim that the vegetables sold at the farmers' market are healthier. It would support an argument that Tyler should go to the farmers' market instead of the supermarket but Zara only suggests they could stop at the market.

C is incorrect. Since produce grown without pesticides might be heathier than produce grown with pesticides, this statement weakens rather than supports Zara's claim.

D is incorrect. This statement is not relevant to the claim that the vegetables sold at farmers' markets are healthier than those sold at supermarkets.

Practice questions

1 A politician says in a town meeting: 'Floods are good for agriculture. They bring sediments and nutrients to the soil so farm crops thrive in the season following a flood.'

Which one of these statements, if true, best supports the politician's claim?

A The whole year's crops can be lost in a flood.

B Climate change has made floods more sudden.

C Floods move topsoil so a farm could lose all its productive soil.

D Floods refill aquifers and farm dams.

2 An environmentalist said in a television interview: 'Australian species are facing extreme habitat loss. We need to protect and restore Australian bush and establish safe havens so that native species can begin to rebuild their populations.'

Which one of these statements, if true, best supports the environmentalist's claim?

A Scientists are conducting wildlife surveys.

B Every two minutes Australia loses an MCG-sized area of forest and bushland.

C People enjoy seeing native wildlife in its natural habitat.

D A new wildlife sanctuary is being created.

Identifying additional evidence to weaken an argument

- When someone makes a claim they provide reasons to support their claim. Any statement that calls into question or contradicts any of the evidence used to support the claim will weaken the claim.
- First identify the claim and the supporting evidence. Then assess which of the statements undermines or contradicts the supporting evidence or gives reasons why the claim is not valid.

Look for the following:

- any statement that contradicts the evidence in the claim
- any statement that undermines the accuracy of the claim
- any statement that undermines or limits the scope of the claim
- any statement that makes the claim less likely to hold up.

Read the questions below carefully. When working out your answers, eliminate any that are incorrect until you find the answer that is correct.

SAMPLE QUESTION

Zelda wants to attend Acro (Acrobatics) dance classes. Her parents have said no for this year because they think Acro might be dangerous. Zelda says she has done forward rolls, handsprings, handstands and cartwheels in gymnastics without hurting herself and Acro will be no different.

Which one of these statements, if true, most **weakens** Zelda's parents' argument?

A Acro increases strength and flexibility.

B Typical Acro injuries include wrist fractures, ankle sprains, and knee and lower back pain.

C The Acro classes clash with Zelda's gymnastics classes so she will need to give up gymnastics to take up Acro.

D The Acro teacher is certified in safe training practices.

D is correct. Zelda's parents' argument is that Acro is dangerous. Any statement that suggests Acro dancing can be safe will weaken their claim or argument. The fact that the Acro teacher is certified in safe training practices weakens the parents' argument.

A is incorrect. Zelda's parents' argument is that Acro might be dangerous. The statement that Acro increases strength and flexibility supports Acro as an activity but neither strengthens nor weakens Zelda's parents' argument that Acro is dangerous.

B is incorrect. The statement that typical Acro injuries include wrist fractures, ankle sprains, and knee and lower back pain supports Zelda's parent's argument.

C is incorrect. This statement that Acro classes clash with Zelda's gymnastics neither supports not weakens Zelda's parents' argument.

 Practice questions

1 Hula hoops are great fun and good exercise. Hooping develops fitness, balance and coordination.

Which one of these statements, if true, most **weakens** the above argument?

A Hooping fitness classes are held in many parts of the world.

B Most people struggle to manage hooping effectively.

C Hoops have been used since 500 BC but weren't named hula hoops until the 1950s.

D Modern-day hoops are made of plastic.

2 Archie and his cousins are having a discussion.

Archie: 'We'd better not drive to Old Pa's on Friday because the Bureau of Meteorology has said it might rain on Friday. It's a two-hour drive and I don't like driving in the rain.'

Which one of these statements, if true, most **weakens** Archie's argument?

A **Linus:** 'We need to be there for Old Pa's 90th birthday on Saturday.'

B **Ariana:** 'Old Pa loves birthday celebrations.'

C **Rose:** 'The Bureau of Meteorology only said it might rain on Friday, not that it will definitely rain all day.'

D **Niall:** 'The Bureau of Meteorology is very accurate with its predictions.'

    ☞ **Answers and explanations on pages 61–62**

Answering questions about differences in travel times

■ To answer questions that involve travel times you must be confident in converting minutes and hours, and in writing decimal portions and fractions of hours as minutes. For example, 1.25 hours = 1 hour and 15 minutes. There is a small table below that includes some important conversions. You can create your own and add more to it.

Decimal (hours)	Fraction (hours)	Minutes
0.25	$\frac{1}{4}$	15
0.333 3333	$\frac{1}{3}$	20
0.5	$\frac{1}{2}$	30
0.666 6666	$\frac{2}{3}$	40
0.75	$\frac{3}{4}$	45
1	1	60

■ It is also important to know how speed, distance and time are related. If Train A is two times as fast as Train B, it will take one-half of the time it takes Train B to cover the same distance. Also, if they travel for the same time, Train A will cover two times the distance.

■ Drawing simple arrows to represent trains or cars can be very useful when answering questions about travel times.

SAMPLE QUESTION

A slow train departed Paddington station at 2 pm and arrived at its destination at 6.30 pm. A second train departed Paddington, travelling three times as fast, and arrived at the same destination at the same time. If both trains were travelling at a constant speed and did not stop at all, what time did the second train depart?

A 4.30 pm   B 4.50 pm

C 5.00 pm   D 5.30 pm

C is correct. Remember that 1.5 hours = 1 hour 30 minutes. The difference between 6.30 pm and 2 pm is 4 hours and 30 minutes (6.5 − 2 = 4.5).

If the second train is three times faster, it will do the trip in one-third of the time. So we can divide the trip into three sections of equal time (4.5 hours ÷ 3 = 1.5 hours). It will take the second train 1.5 hours to reach the destination. This means the train departed 1.5 hours before it arrived at 6.30 pm (6.5 hours − 1.5 = 5). The train departed Paddington at 5.00 pm.

You could draw arrows to represent the difference in time taken, as shown below. This may help with some of the more difficult questions.

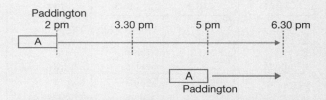

Practice questions

1 A high-speed train proposed for Australia will reduce the 3-hour travel time between Sydney and Canberra to 45 minutes. If it currently takes 10 hours to travel between Sydney and Melbourne, how long would it take a high-speed train to do the same trip?

A 2 hours 15 minutes

B 2 hours 30 minutes

C 2 hours 50 minutes

D 3 hours

2 Every morning Jeremy runs to the harbour and then walks home the way he came. It takes Jeremy 20 minutes to run from his house to the harbour. He runs three times as fast as he walks. If he leaves his house at 6 am, at what time does he arrive back home?

A 6.40 am   B 7.00 am

C 7.20 am   D 8.00 am

Selecting items from a number of lists

- Many questions will require you to use a process of elimination to decide which items from a list can or cannot be chosen. The way to solve these is best explained with a question. Look at the sample question below then read the explanation. This form of process of elimination is usually the way to solve problems of this type.
- Use your pencil to cross out items or to circle items on the lists. This allows you to focus on one bit of information at a time without trying to keep all parts of the question in your head.

SAMPLE QUESTION

At a music camp, Luciano must choose four courses to participate in. He must choose one course from each list.

List 1	List 2	List 3	List 4
Major Scales	Power Chords	Honky-tonk	The Blues
Key Changes	The Blues	Major Scales	Power Chords
Opera	80s Ballads	Minor Scales	Key Changes
Rock'n'roll	Pipe Bands	Opera	Minor Scales

Luciano knows he will choose The Blues, Pipe Bands and Minor Scales.

Which of the following courses will he **not** be able to choose as his final course?

A Rock'n'roll   B Major Scales
C Opera   D Power Chords

D is correct. Luciano cannot choose Power Chords.
Usually, one of the chosen courses will appear in one or two lists only. Find the chosen course that appears in the fewest lists. This will help to figure out which course must be chosen from which list. In this case Luciano can only choose Pipe Bands in List 2. It is not available in any other list so it must be chosen from List 2. Circle Pipe Bands and cross off the rest of the list.

This means that The Blues, which is only available in List 2 and List 4, must be chosen from List 4. Circle it and cross off the rest of the list.

Minor Scales, which is available in List 3 and List 4, must be chosen in List 3. Circle it and cross off the rest of the list.

The fourth course must be chosen from List 1. Power Chords does not appear in List 1 so Luciano cannot choose it.

Practice questions

1 At a writer's retreat, Ben could choose four courses in which to participate. He had to choose one course from each session.

Session 1	Session 2	Session 3	Session 4
Short Stories	Young Adult	Children's Books	Non-fiction
Crime	Children's Books	Romance	Essay Writing
Romance	Graphic Novels	Short Stories	Crime
Non-fiction	Biographies	Historical Fiction	Graphic Novels

Ben wants to learn how to write about Crime, Graphic Novels and Biographies. Which of the following courses can Ben **definitely not** also choose?

A Historical Fiction   B Romance
C Short Stories   D Non-fiction

2 At a sporting festival Celia can choose to hear speeches made by sportspeople in four different sessions. Celia must choose one sportsperson from each session.

Session 1	Session 2	Session 3	Session 4
Samantha Kerr	Liz Ellis	Adam Goodes	Patty Mills
Patty Mills	Tim Cahill	Steve Waugh	Adam Goodes
Dawn Fraser	Steve Waugh	Lauren Jackson	Liz Ellis
Tim Cahill	Lauren Jackson	Jessica Fox	Greg Norman

Celia chose to hear Jessica Fox, Patty Mills and Steve Waugh speak. Who is it **not possible** for her to also choose?

A Liz Ellis   B Tim Cahill
C Lauren Jackson   D Dawn Fraser

Deciding how many days or events lie between specific dates

- To answer questions involving dates it is important to know the number of days in each month. Make sure you know these or have a method to work it out very quickly (look up the knuckle mnemonic method). A 28-day February is exactly four weeks, while a 30-day or 31-day month is two or three days more than that.

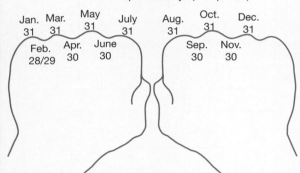

Knuckles = 31 days
Dips = 30 days (except Feb)

Jan. 31 Mar. 31 May 31 July 31 Aug. 31 Oct. 31 Dec. 31
Feb. 28/29 Apr. 30 June 30 Sep. 30 Nov. 30

- Depending on the question the first and last days in a period of time will be included, so be sure to include them in any calculations. For example, a performance that runs 'from Wednesday 10th to Wednesday 17th' usually means it runs for 8 days, not one week, as there are performances on both Wednesdays.
- You can also sketch very simple calendars to help you with these questions.

> 30 days has September, April, June and November. All the rest have 31 except February alone, which has 28 days clear and 29 in a leap year.

SAMPLE QUESTION

Jimmy meets his brother every Monday and Thursday to play tennis, unless it is raining. This year, May started on a Sunday and it rained consistently from the 15th to the 18th. **H**ow many times did Jimmy play tennis with his brother in May?

A 7 **B** 8 **C** 9 **D** 10

B is correct. Jimmy and his brother played tennis 8 times in May.

May has 31 days and starts on a Sunday. Without the rain, Jimmy will play twice a week for four weeks and then once on Monday 30th. If the 1st is a Sunday, then 14 days (2 weeks) after that is Sunday 15th. The rain knocks out Monday 16th for that week. So the number of times he plays tennis is given by:

4 weeks × 2 sessions
+ 1 extra Monday − 1 rained out = 8

You can see it more clearly on the sketched calendar below. The rainy days are crossed out. The days Jimmy plays tennis are circled. Notice that it isn't necessary to write all the dates in.

Su	M	Tu	W	Th	F	Sa
1	②	3	4	⑤	6	7
8	⑨	10	11	⑫	13	14
~~15~~	⑯	~~17~~	~~18~~	⑲	20	21
22	㉓	24	25	㉖	27	28
29	㉚	31	1	2	3	4

Practice questions

1 Virat plays cricket four times a week on Monday, Wednesday, Thursday and Saturday. If January starts on a Saturday, how many times does Virat play cricket in January?

A 15 **B** 16
C 17 **D** 18

2 An orchestra is playing at the Sydney Opera House. The orchestra will perform every night of the week except Monday and will play two shows on each Saturday and Sunday. The first performance is on Wednesday 23 November and the final performance is on the evening of Saturday 17 December. How many performances will there be?

A 24 **B** 27
C 29 **D** 31

Arranging shapes so they fit together

- Thinking about how pieces of a puzzle fit together is a great test of your problem-solving skills. Pentominoes, shapes made by joining five squares, are commonly used in some tests.
- While the questions here are printed on paper, the key to solving questions like this is to familiarise yourself with these shapes in the real world. Cut out some pentominoes and see how they fit together with one another.
- Some shapes will not fit together on a grid without leaving gaps that cannot then be filled. Some shapes must be placed in the centre, some at the edges and others in a corner. Make sure you know which ones can fit where.

SAMPLE QUESTION

Four shapes are needed to cover the 4-by-5 grid below. They can be placed anywhere on the grid and can be rotated and reflected.

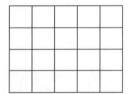

The following shape must be used twice.

Which other two shapes **cannot** now be used to cover the grid completely?

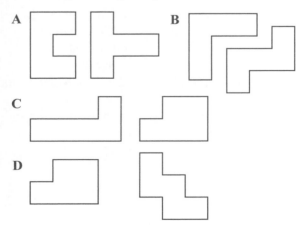

D is correct. The shape that is used twice must be placed with its flat side against the side of the grid. If it isn't, it will leave an unfillable gap. For example:

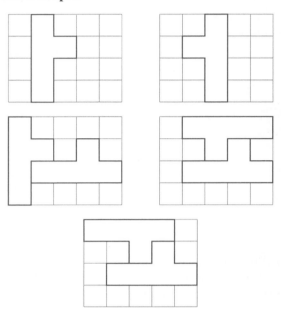

If 1, 2, 3 or 4 squares are left to be filled, we know a pentomino (made from 5 squares) will be too big to fit.

Once you place one against the side of the grid, the other only has a couple of places to fit. Once this is done, it becomes clear that the second shape in D, that looks like a staircase, will not fit into the grid without leaving unfillable gaps.

Some possible solutions for the other options are shown below. There is no solution for D.

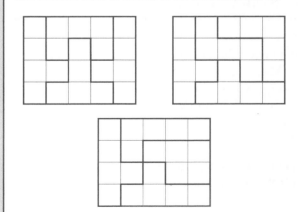

Arranging shapes so they fit together

Practice questions

1 The shape below must be one of three shapes used to cover the grid.

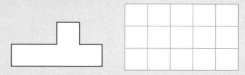

If the other two shapes must be identical, which shape **must** be used?

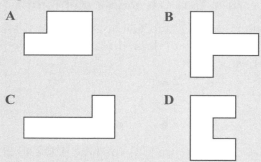

2 Three shapes are needed to cover the grid entirely. The shape below is used twice.

Which **cannot** be the third shape? The shapes may be rotated and reflected.

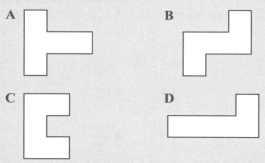

Answering questions involving the directions on a compass

- Always draw a compass in the corner of your page to help you answer these questions. Your compass could look like this:

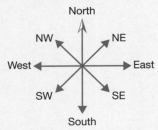

- Remember that the direction of Town X from Town Y is the reverse of Town Y from Town X. That is, if Town X is north of Town Y, then Town Y is south of Town X.

- When sketching, use points to mark towns or people and only draw what you know must be true.

- Some questions will give directions only, without giving distances. In these cases, it is usually assumed the distances between towns are fairly similar. Remembering this will help you when sketching a map.

- Unless otherwise specified, north is towards the top of the page on maps and this is the case in all questions in this book.

- If one town is **due south** (or north, west, east) of another, it means it is **directly** south, not just further south. Some questions will specify this to avoid confusion but many will just use **south** to indicate this.

Town A is south of Town B and west of Town C. Town B is south of Town E and west of Town D. Which option best describes the direction of Town D from Town A?

A north

B north-west

C north-east

D east

C is correct. Town D is north-east of Town A.

The first sentence tells you how A, B and C are related. A sketch of those three towns may look like this:

B ●

A ●   ● C

The second sentence tells you how B, D and E are related. A final sketch of the area could look like this:

E ●

B ●   ● D

A ●   ● C

The question asks in which direction Town D is from Town A. Place the tip of your pencil on A and draw an arrow to D. What direction is this arrow?

E ●

B ●   ● D

A ●   ● C

Town D is north-east of Town A.

Answering questions involving the directions on a compass

 Practice questions

1 There are five cities in a country. Derby is north-east of Albany, Chester is south-west of Ealing, Boothby is due south of Albany and Chester is south-east of Derby.

Which city is furthest to the east?

A Albany

B Chester

C Derby

D Ealing

2 In a regional area, the following is known.

Town A is directly west of Town C.

Town D is directly south of Town A.

Town C is directly north of Town B.

Town D is directly west of Town E.

Which of the following diagrams is **not** a possible view of the area?

A ● Town A   ● Town C

● Town D   ● Town B   ● Town E

B ● Town A   ● Town C

● Town D   ● Town E   ● Town B

C ● Town A   ● Town C

● Town B

● Town D   ● Town E

D ● Town A   ● Town C

● Town D   ● Town B   ● Town E

☞ **Answers and explanations on page 63**

Answering questions involving different views of the same object

- There are many variations of questions that involve deciding if a particular view is or isn't a view of a given object.
- If a question involves a floorplan, as the sample question here does, count the number of rooms, note the shape of the rooms and observe how they fit together. Use a process of elimination to decide the answer as this will usually be the best method.
- If the question involves cubes, it can be useful to shade all the faces that can be seen from the top in one colour or pattern and all the faces that can be seen from the side in another colour or pattern. This can help count the number of squares visible from particular views.

SAMPLE QUESTION

The following is a view of a single-storey building.

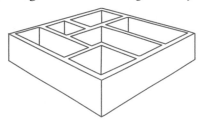

Which of the following represents a floorplan of the building?

A 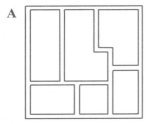   B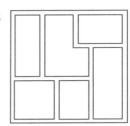

C 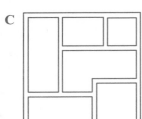   D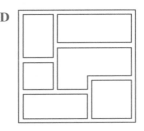

D is correct.

Studying the 3D image in the question we note that, of the six rooms, only one is L-shaped.

A is incorrect. It has two L-shaped rooms.

Of the other five rooms, there is only one square room. **C is incorrect.** It has two square rooms.

B is incorrect. The square room sits inside the corner of the L-shaped room.

D must be the correct answer. Check to see that it matches.

Practice questions

1. The following is a view of a single-storey building. The building is rectangular. It has one side longer than the other and is made up of four rooms.

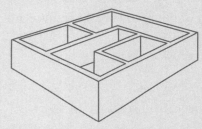

Which of the following represents a floorplan of the building?

A 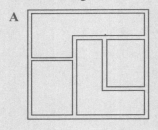   B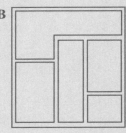

C 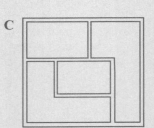   D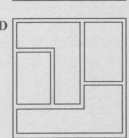

Answering questions involving different views of the same object

2 Seven cubes are attached to create the solid below.

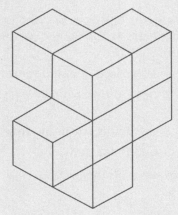

Which is **not** a possible view of the solid?

A   B

C   D

Ordering items in a row or around a table

- Many questions require finding which of a number of items or people have a particular characteristic. Information will relate the position of items to each other and to the characteristic. Read all information before attempting this sort of question.
- When items are placed in a row it matters which items are placed at the end of each row. When items are arranged in a circle there is no start or end to the circle, so it does not matter where the first item is placed. Remember this when arranging items in a circle.
- Keep in mind that an item that is one space away from another is next to it. So an item that is two spaces away from another is next to it but one. For example, if Max is sitting between Helen and Gloria, then Helen is two spaces from Gloria, even though there is only one person between them.

SAMPLE QUESTION

Five pilots—Maverick, Iceman, Rooster, Phoenix and Fanboy—are each flying a plane in a single-row formation. All are flying grey planes except for one who is flying a silver plane.

Fanboy is flying next to Phoenix, who is two spaces from Maverick. Rooster is two spaces from Maverick. If the silver plane is three spaces away from Iceman, who is flying the silver plane?

A Maverick   B Rooster
C Fanboy   D Phoenix

D is correct. Phoenix is flying the silver plane.

Maverick is two spaces from two different pilots therefore he must be in the middle of the row of five. Phoenix and Rooster, the pilots who are two spaces from Maverick, must then be on the ends of the row. Fanboy is next to Phoenix, which means Iceman is next to Rooster. The silver plane is three spaces from Iceman and Phoenix must be the pilot. The two possible arrangements are:

Rooster   Iceman → Maverick → Fanboy → **Phoenix**

Phoenix ← Fanboy ← Maverick ← Iceman   Rooster

Notice that sometimes the order will not be definite.

Practice questions

1 A prize is in one of five boxes labelled A, B, C, D and E that are mixed up and put in a row from left to right.
- Box A is two spaces from the prize.
- Box C is next to Box D and two spaces from Box E.
- Box B is on the far left of the row.
- Box E is on the far right.

Which box contains the prize?

A Box B

B Box C

C Box D

D Box E

2 One green, one blue, two red and two yellow beads are evenly spaced around a bracelet. The green bead is not next to a yellow bead. The yellow beads are not next to each other.

Which of the following **cannot** be true?

A The blue bead is next to a red bead.

B The blue bead is opposite the green bead.

C The blue bead is between two yellow beads.

D The blue bead is next to the green bead.

Answering questions with nets, dice and dominoes

■ To prepare for questions about nets of dice, it is a good idea to cut out some nets yourself and fold them up. Get comfortable with which faces of a net will be next to each other and which faces will be opposite each other. This will help you better visualise the nets in a test situation.

■ When the faces of dice are images, take note of important features. For example, if one of the corners of a triangle is pointing to a particular face, make sure you know which face it is or isn't. This method is important in answering the sample question below.

SAMPLE QUESTION

The following is a view of a six-sided dice.

Which is the only possible net of the dice?

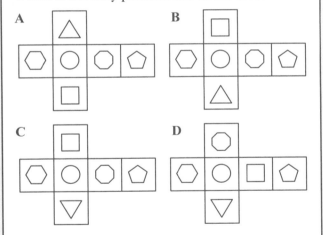

C is correct.
A is incorrect. If A were folded to make a dice, and the dice placed so that the triangle was on top, the octagon would be to the right of the circle not the left.
B is incorrect. If B were folded, one of the points of the triangle would be pointing at the circle, which is not the case.
D is incorrect. D has all three shapes connected in a row so we could not see them all at once, as the triangle would be on the side opposite the octagon.

 Practice questions

1 The following net is folded into a six-sided dice.

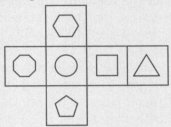

Which of the following is **not** a possible view of the dice?

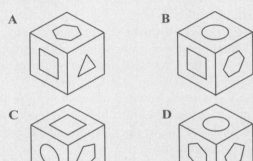

2 The following net is folded into a dice.

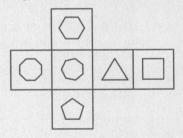

In a game, two such dice are rolled and the number of sides on the shape shown on each dice are multiplied together to get a score. What is the difference between the minimum and maximum scores possible?

A 10
B 48
C 55
D 63

☞ Answers and explanations on page 64

Identifying what is true or what cannot be true when people are placed in a row

- Many questions will ask you to draw conclusions after placing people or items in a row. The focus here is on questions that require you to identify which statement must be true or cannot be true.
- In order to draw a conclusion you must read all information in the question carefully, identifying which bits of information can be acted on immediately (e.g. 'Tim is furthest to the right') and which bits can only be taken into consideration once other people or items are set in place (e.g. 'Minka sat to the left of Kelly').
- It is also important to infer your own information. For example, if you are told that Beni is further left than Paula, you know that Paula must be to the right of Beni.
- In some instances, drawing a very quick sketch using letters or shapes to represent each person (or item) can help you visualise the question and means you don't have to retain all bits of information at once. You can work on the question one step at a time. Once you have sketched the possible order of the items, you can answer any question about them.

SAMPLE QUESTION

Four cards are dealt out in a row. The Ace is further right than the Queen and the Jack is directly next to the King. If the Jack is further left than the Queen, which sentence **must be true**?

A The Jack is furthest left.

B The King is furthest left.

C The Ace is furthest right.

D The Queen is furthest right.

C is correct. If the Jack is further left than the Queen, then the King must also be further left than the Queen as it is directly next to the Jack. We can treat the Jack and King as one unit and place them to the left of the Queen, with the Ace to the Queen's right. The two possible orders are below.

JK – Q – A
KJ – Q – A

A and B are incorrect. They are possible but not necessarily true.

D is incorrect. It is never true that the Queen is furthest to the right.

 Practice questions

❶ Jan, Ben and Mo are standing in a row. If Jan is to the left of Mo and Ben is to the right of Jan, which of the following statements **must be true**?

A Jan is furthest to the left.

B Ben is in the middle.

C Mo is in the middle.

D Ben is furthest to the right.

❷ The names of four SRC candidates were drawn from a hat to indicate the order in which they would speak. Calista was not drawn first, Bryan was drawn before Graham, and Heather was drawn after Calista. Which of the following statements **must be true**?

A Graham will be last to speak.

B Heather will speak after Graham.

C Graham will speak second.

D Bryan will speak first.

1 Four shapes are to be chosen to fill the 4-by-5 grid shown below. The shapes can be rotated and reflected. The shape below must be used.

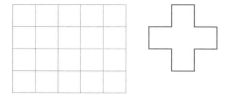

Which three other shapes can be used to cover the rectangle?

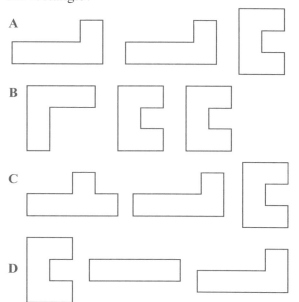

A

B

C

D

2 'Whenever Owen's mother earns a bonus at work, she takes Owen shopping on Saturday to choose a book to buy.'

Natalie: 'Owen brought a new book to school on Monday. His mother must have earned a bonus last week.'

Troy: 'If Owen's mother gets a bonus this week, Owen is sure to get a new book this Saturday.'

If the information in the box is true, whose reasoning is correct?

A Natalie only

B Troy only

C Both Natalie and Troy

D Neither Natalie nor Troy

3 Maggie walks to school with her friends Tori and Kotaro except when it rains or on Thursdays when she has to go to Before School Care. Her mother starts work early on Thursdays and doesn't like to leave Maggie alone in the unit so she drives her to Before School Care.

If all the above statements are true, only one of the sentences below **cannot** be true. Which one?

A It was sunny on Tuesday so Maggie did not go to school by car.

B It rained on Thursday so Maggie went to school by car.

C It rained on Wednesday so Maggie went to school by car.

D It did not rain on Friday so Maggie went to school by car.

4 Town A is north of Town B, Town C is north of Town D, and Town C is east of Town B. In which direction would I travel to get from Town D to Town B?

A west

B north-west

C north

D north-east

5 Tu, Iris and Dean love making big bowls of fruit salad. Tu likes to use kiwi fruit, mango, banana, blueberries and pineapple. Dean likes to use banana, orange and pear. Iris likes to use peach, kiwi fruit, orange, banana and pineapple.

Which fruit does Tu like to use in fruit salad that neither Dean nor Iris likes to use?

A orange and peach

B peach and banana

C mango and blueberries

D pear and mango

6 Which two dominoes from the five below will complete the circuit of dominoes below?

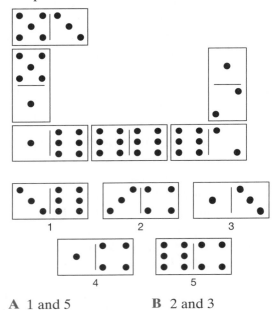

A 1 and 5
B 2 and 3
C 2 and 4
D 3 and 4

7 Oli, Will and Jack are the only three students standing in the canteen line. If Jack is ahead of Will and Will is not ahead of Oli, which of the following statements must be true?

A Oli is second in line.

B Jack is at the front of the line.

C Will is second in line.

D Will is third in line.

8 A naturalist says: 'Bogong moths are a species in danger of extinction due to drought, pesticide use and climate change. Their larvae grow in the soil. Adult moths travel thousands of kilometres each spring to the Snowy Mountains. Bogongs provide essential food for pygmy possums that hibernate during winter and then feast on bogongs in spring. It's vital that action is taken to protect bogong moths.'

Which one of these statements, if true, best supports the naturalist's claim?

A Without Bogong moths to eat, pygmy possums will become extinct.

B Bogong months are a species in danger of extinction.

C Strong environmental laws are needed to protect ecosystems.

D It's vital that action is taken to protect Bogong moths.

9 Aisha is on her way to school when she sees her friend Leon walking across the road.

Aisha: 'Leon had better get off the road! There's a truck coming!'

Which of the following assumptions is needed for Aisha's conclusion to work?

A Aisha likes trucks.

B Leon must get off the road.

C The truck is a toy.

D The truck is not going to stop.

☞ Answers and explanations on pages 65–66

SAMPLE TEST 1A

10 Colin had to choose four subjects to study. He must choose one subject from each list below.

List 1	List 2	List 3	List 4
Art	Logic	Music	Woodwork
English	French	Cooking	French
Music	Woodwork	English	Art
Logic	Sewing	Computers	Sewing

Which combination of subjects is it **not possible** for Colin to choose?

A Computers, Art, Woodwork, Sewing

B English, French, Woodwork, Sewing

C Music, French, Logic, Cooking

D Art, English, French, Logic

11 'You really should get an ebike. There are so many reasons for buying one. Using an ebike is fun. An ebike uses battery power to help you cycle further or faster and go up hills more easily than using a regular bicycle. In spite of the battery power, ebikes do also help to keep you fit. Using an ebike is a great way to get to work or school. They are also kinder to the planet than using a petrol or diesel car. I highly recommend you get an ebike!'

Which statement best expresses the main idea in the above text?

A Ebikes are kinder to the planet than petrol or diesel cars.

B An ebike is a great way to get to work or school.

C Get an ebike!

D Ebikes are fun.

12 Raptors are a special group of birds also known as birds of prey. They include hawks, owls, condors, eagles, falcons and vultures. Birds of prey are apex predators that hunt and feed on other animals. They have sharp vision to detect and catch their prey, such as fish, rabbits, lizards and rodents.

Which statement best expresses the main idea of the text?

A Birds of prey hunt and feed on animals.

B Eagles are raptors.

C Raptors are birds of prey.

D Raptors often catch their prey during flight.

13 A movie is to be shown at a cinema from Tuesday 3rd to Monday 16th of the same month. It will be shown once each day except on Fridays and Saturdays when it will be shown twice both days. How many times will the movie be shown at the cinema?

A 16   B 17   C 18   D 19

14 When Jack signed up for bouldering lessons, he wanted to climb a wall that was graded V3. His instructor told him: 'That's a demanding climb! We test climbers before they can move onto climbs V3 and higher. To have even a chance of passing the test, you must have successfully climbed all walls in the V0 to V2 range.'

If Jack's instructor is correct, which one of these statements will be true?

A None of the climbers who have not climbed all walls in the V0 to V2 range will be allowed to climb V3 walls.

B Only the climbers who have not climbed all walls in the V0 to V2 range will be allowed to climb V3 walls.

C All of the climbers who have climbed all walls in the V0 to V2 range will be allowed to climb V3 walls.

D Some of the climbers who have not climbed all walls in the V0 to V2 range will be allowed to climb V3 walls.

15 A square piece of paper is folded in half to create a rectangle. This rectangle is folded in half to create a square. These two steps are repeated once, resulting in a square with sides of 5 cm.

What is the side length of the original piece of paper?

A 10 cm   B 20 cm   C 40 cm   D 80 cm

1 Thelma and Louise are going on a road trip and are going to share the driving. Thelma likes driving more than Louise does so she is going to drive for twice as long as Louise. They drive from 8 am to 6 pm on the same day, only stopping to change drivers once. If Louise drives first, at what time does Thelma take the wheel?

A 10.30 am **B** 11.20 am
C 12 midday **D** 2.40 pm

2 To be allowed to go to the party on Saturday, Lavinia knows she has to make sure her parents are happy with her behaviour. One way to make her parents happy with her behaviour is to tidy her room and wash the dog.

Gabriel: 'If Lavinia goes to the party she must have tidied her room and washed the dog.'

Tao: 'If Lavinia doesn't go to the party she can't have tidied her room or washed the dog.'

Whose reasoning is correct?

A Gabriel only
B Tao only
C Both Gabriel and Tao
D Neither Gabriel nor Tao

3 Town A is west of Town E and north of Town B. Town B is east of Town D. Town C is south of Town B. Town F is south of Town E and east of Town B. Which town is north-west of Town C?

A Town A **B** Town B
C Town D **D** Town F

4 Stan and Rina are outside the classroom.

Stan: 'Melody wants me to take her school backpack to the library for her. She says it has a red ribbon tied to the strap.'

Rina: 'Here's a backpack with a red ribbon tied to the strap. It has to be Melody's'.

Which one of the following shows the mistake Rina has made?

A Just because the backpack has a red ribbon tied to its strap, it does not mean it has to be Melody's.

B Melody might be trying to steal someone else's backpack.

C The ribbon on the backpack might not be the right colour.

D Melody might not be in the library when Rina and Stan get there.

5 Peyton, Zianna, Caitlyn and Ariana are competing as a team in the 4 × 50 m relay at the swimming carnival. If Caitlyn is swimming before Ariana, Ariana is swimming after Peyton, and Zianna is swimming before Peyton, which of the following statements must be true?

A Zianna is swimming first.
B Peyton is swimming third.
C Ariana is swimming fourth.
D Caitlyn is swimming second.

6 On a stringed instrument, if a string is halved in length, the note that is made by playing it will be higher by one octave. A string that is 32 cm in length is played to make a note. If the length of the string is decreased to 8 cm, what change will be heard in the note?

A The note will be 2 octaves higher.

B The note will be 2 octaves lower.

C The note will be 4 octaves higher.

D The note will be 4 octaves lower.

7

Harry: 'If your electric blanket catches fire, you can use any of the extinguishers.'

Jakob: 'If you have a wood fire and the fire gets out of control, I think you have to use the AB(E) extinguisher.'

Mira: 'You can use the AB(E) extinguisher in the kitchen if you have been frying chips and they catch fire.'

Millicent: 'You should use an AB(E) extinguisher if the curtains catch fire from a burning candle.'

If the information above is true, whose reasoning is correct?

A Mira and Harry

B Millicent and Jacob

C Jacob and Mira

D Millicent and Harry

8 Ann, Bea, Cam, Don, El and Flo are sitting evenly spaced around a circular table. Ann is sitting directly opposite Don and Bea is not sitting next to El.

Who **cannot** be seated next to Cam?

A Ann   B Bea   C El   D Flo

9 Carrots are full of vitamins and minerals and fibre. They are good for your eyes, your heart and your immune system. They are also good for preventing cancer because they contain antioxidants, the phytonutrients that help your body fight diseases. Add some carrots to your diet every day.

Which one of these statements, if true, most **weakens** the above argument?

A Carrots are popular snack foods, either on their own or with dips.

B Carrots are good for your eyes, your heart and your immune system.

C Carrot allergies are rare but some people may have an allergic reaction to carrots.

D Carrots are good for you raw or cooked.

10 The dominoes are to be arranged in a rectangle so that no number is placed next to itself.

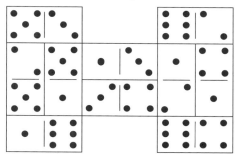

Which combination of two dominoes **cannot** be used to complete the rectangle?

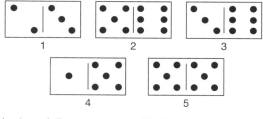

A 1 and 5   B 1 and 4
C 2 and 3   D 2 and 4

☞ Answers and explanations on pages 66–68

11 Claudia makes a salad with lettuce, olives, tomato, cucumber, radishes and capsicum. Miley makes a salad with lettuce, parsley, tomato, cucumber, olives, red onion, capsicum and roast pumpkin. Greg makes a salad with lettuce, tomato, grated carrot, cucumber, red onion and capsicum.

Which ingredients does Miley use that neither Greg nor Claudia uses?

A olives and parsley

B red onion and radishes

C grated carrot and olives

D parsley and roast pumpkin

12 School holidays begin on Saturday 9 and end on Sunday 24 of the same month. Jimmy makes a visit to his grandparents on Mondays, Wednesdays, Saturdays and Sundays during his school holidays. How many visits will he make?

A 10

B 11

C 12

D 13

13 Djurdja's mother works at the office three days a week and at home two days a week. When she works at the office, she takes a packed lunch. Last Monday she took a salad, a cookie, cheese and crackers, an apple and a banana. On Wednesday she took a sandwich, a banana and an apple. On Friday she took a cookie, leftovers, an apple, trail mix and a banana.

What did Djurdja's mother take on Monday that neither the Wednesday lunchbox nor the Friday lunchbox contained?

A cookie and salad

B salad and cheese and crackers

C trail mix and sandwich

D cheese and crackers and apple

14 A 4-by-5 grid is covered by two shapes as shown below. These shapes cannot be moved.

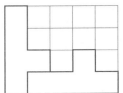

Which other two shapes **cannot** be used to cover the grid? The shapes may be rotated and reflected.

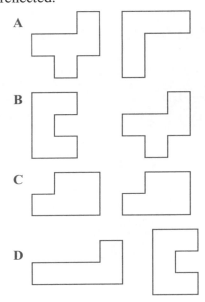

15 To celebrate its 100th birthday, the Green Town fire station has been upgraded. The new design has separate work and living areas, improved recreation spaces and a new training room. There are also separate male and female bathrooms.

Which statement best expresses the main idea of the text?

A The Green Town fire station celebrated its 100th birthday.

B The Green Town fire station received 1200 calls for assistance last year.

C The Green Town fire station now has separate male and female bathrooms.

D The Green Town fire station has been upgraded.

1 Four playing cards are arranged in a row. The King is to the immediate left of the Queen and the Jack is further right than the Ace. Which card is **definitely not** second from the left?

A Ace

B King

C Queen

D Jack

2 The Mona Lisa is one of the most famous and valuable artworks in the world. It was painted by Leonardo da Vinci in about 1503 and is now on display in the Louvre, a famous art gallery in Paris. The Mona Lisa is insured for over $800 million.

Which one of these statements, if true, most **strengthens** the above argument?

A The Mona Lisa is one of the most famous artworks in the world.

B Art critics say the painting is a very lifelike portrait.

C The Mona Lisa is protected by bulletproof glass.

D The Mona Lisa is very small, measuring only 77 cm x 53 cm.

3 The bestselling Harry Potter books were made into successful films because everyone who loved the books wanted to see the movies.

Eli: 'It's true that all bestselling books make highly successful films.'

Which one of the following sentences shows the mistake Eli has made?

A Some people who love a book might be disappointed by the movie.

B Not every popular book is made into a movie.

C Some successful movies are based on a screenplay and not a book.

D Bestselling books are worth reading.

4 Xander walks 200 m south from his starting point, before turning and walking 100 m east, 100 m north, 200 m east, 300 m north, 100 m west, 100 m south, then 200 m west.

In which direction and for how far must he walk to get back to his starting point?

A 200 m south

B 100 m west

C 100 m south

D He is already back at his starting point.

5 Whoever untied Katharine's goat from her backyard clothesline must have had both an opportunity and a motive.

If this is true, which one of these sentences must also be true?

A If Joo did not untie the goat, he must have had an opportunity.

B If Joo untied the goat, he cannot have had an opportunity.

C If Joo did not have a motive, he cannot have been the one to untie the goat.

D If Joo had both an opportunity and a motive, he cannot have untied the goat.

6 At a music camp, Birgitte must choose four instruments to learn about. She must choose one instrument from each list shown below.

List 1	List 2	List 3	List 4
cello	guitar	trumpet	oboe
xylophone	trumpet	percussion	flute
trumpet	trombone	oboe	guitar
flute	violin	clarinet	clarinet

Birgitte chose to learn about percussion, the clarinet and the trumpet. Which of the following instruments did Birgitte **definitely not** choose?

A guitar

B flute

C trombone

D oboe

7 Alex and Maia competed in a cycling race that started at 9 am. Alex completed the race four times faster than Maia. If Maia finished the race at 2 pm, at what time did Alex cross the finish line?

A 9.45 am   **B** 10 am

C 10.15 am   **D** 10.30 am

8

> A blood orange is an orange. A ruby grapefruit is a grapefruit. Both fruits have ruby-coloured flesh. A ruby grapefruit is sweeter than a white grapefruit. A blood orange is not as sweet as a navel orange and more like a grapefruit in flavour with a hint of raspberry.
>
> If your recipe requires a blood orange and you can't get one, you can substitute a ruby grapefruit or use a navel orange with some raspberries for colour and flavour.

If the information in the box is true, whose reasoning is **incorrect**?

Hugo: 'I used a white grapefruit and some raspberries because my recipe needed a blood orange and the result was too sour. I should have used an orange with some raspberries.'

Annchi: 'I need a blood orange so I'll use a white grapefruit for the grapefruit flavour and some strawberries to give the ruby-red colour. That will work.'

A Hugo only

B Annchi only

C Both Hugo and Annchi

D Neither Hugo nor Annchi

9 Zi's dad has said she can choose two friends to take to the movies for her birthday. Zi has four friends she'd like to take: Camilla, Shawn, Yan and Benny. Camilla might be staying at her grandparents' so may not be able to attend. If Camilla is at her grandparents', then Zi will invite Shawn. If Camilla attends, then Yan will be invited and not Benny.

If Shawn is not invited, which of the other friends will be invited?

A Camilla only

B Benny only

C Yan and Benny

D Camilla and Yan

10 The shape below must be one of three shapes used to cover the grid.

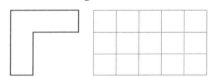

Of the options below, which two other shapes are the only ones that can be used? Shapes may be rotated and reflected.

A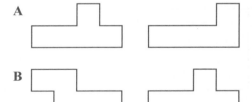

B

C

D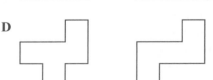

☞ **Answers and explanations on pages 68–70**

11 The local radio station made a community announcement: 'We urge everyone in the area to prepare for bushfire season by making a bushfire survival plan for their home and their family. A well-prepared home makes it easier for firefighters and is also much more likely to survive a bushfire.'

Which one of these statements, if true, best supports the radio station's claim?

A Having a bushfire survival plan can save lives.

B Preparing a survival plan takes as little as five minutes using an online tool.

C There have been higher levels of rainfall leading up to bushfire season.

D The radio station has more information about bushfires on their website.

12

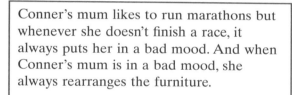

Conner's mum likes to run marathons but whenever she doesn't finish a race, it always puts her in a bad mood. And when Conner's mum is in a bad mood, she always rearranges the furniture.

Saane: 'Your mum rearranged the furniture last week—she must have been in a marathon but didn't finish!'

Conner: 'If Mum doesn't finish the marathon on Saturday, she's sure to rearrange the furniture again!'

If the information in the box is true, whose reasoning is correct?

A Saane only

B Conner only

C Both Saane and Conner

D Neither Saane nor Conner

13 The following is a view of a single-storey building.

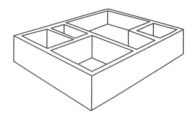

Which of the following represents a floorplan of the building?

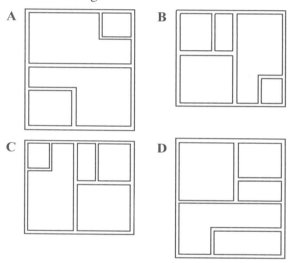

14 Felicity says: 'The oceans are filled with plastic rubbish. We must remove it.'

Which assumption has Felicity made to draw her conclusion?

A We must remove plastic rubbish from the oceans.

B The oceans are filled with plastic rubbish.

C Removing plastic from the oceans would be a good thing.

D We cannot remove all the plastic rubbish from the oceans.

15 Lila, Matt, Nala, Orla, Quin and Peta are sitting evenly spaced around a circular table. Lila is separated from Matt by one person and Quin is directly opposite Nala.

Who **cannot** be seated next to Peta?

A Orla   **B** Nala   **C** Matt   **D** Quin

SAMPLE TEST 2B

15 MIN

1 At a school fete, four stations are set up and different games are played at each. Students do not have to pick one activity from each station. They are free to go to any station at any time. If Toyah wants to play Hopscotch, Finska, Quoits and Petanque, which game must she play at midday?

	Station 1	Station 2	Station 3	Station 4
11 am	Quoits	Twister	French Cricket	Hopscotch
Midday	Red Rover	Hopscotch	Finska	Petanque
1 pm	Finska	Red Rover	Jumbo Jenga	Sticks
2 pm	French Cricket	Petanque	Twister	Finska

A Red Rover

B Hopscotch

C Finska

D Petanque

2 When Mr Xu calls orchestra members to practice it could be for the whole orchestra including strings and brass, or it could be for the string section of the orchestra only or the brass section of the orchestra only. Practices can be called any day of the week but the string section never practises two days in a row.

If all the above statements are true, only one of the sentences below **cannot** be true. Which one?

A If Mr Xu calls practices for Monday and Tuesday, it won't be for strings only.

B If Mr Xu calls practices for Tuesday and Thursday, it could be for strings and/or the whole orchestra.

C If Mr Xu calls practices for Tuesday and Wednesday, it could be for the whole orchestra.

D If Mr Xu calls practices for Monday and Tuesday, you know it could be for the brass section.

3 Bree and Fleur left their homes to meet in town. Both walked at the same speed, made no stops and arrived in town at 2 pm. If Bree lives five times as far from town as Fleur and Bree left home at 1 pm, what time did Fleur leave her home?

A 1.12 pm

B 1.40 pm

C 1.48 pm

D 1.50 pm

4

Mum: 'If you want to have time for horseriding this weekend, you need to get all your homework completed by Friday night. That means you'll need to do homework for at least one hour every night from Monday to Thursday.'

Tori: 'I promise to do one hour every night from Monday to Thursday so I will definitely get all my homework done by Friday.'

Which one of these sentences shows the mistake Tori has made?

A It takes at least one hour per weeknight to get through the homework.

B Doing one hour every night from Monday to Thursday does not ensure the work will be completed on time.

C Doing homework every night from Monday to Thursday ensures the work will be completed by Friday.

D Tori knows her teacher sets too much homework for the class.

☞ Answers and explanations on pages 70–71

SAMPLE TEST 2B

5 Jen, Til, Poppy, Bec and Kim are staying in a motel in rooms 1 to 5.

Jen is next to Til, Poppy is three rooms from Bec, and Kim is two rooms from Jen. Of the four people below, who **cannot** be in room number 1?

A Til

B Kim

C Bec

D Poppy

6 The following is a view of a single-storey building.

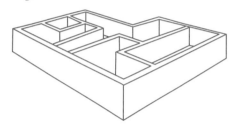

Which of the following represents a floorplan of the building?

A 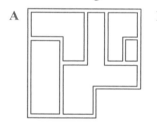 B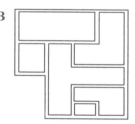

C 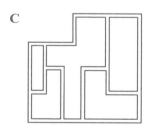 D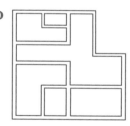

7 Herbs and spices make tasty and healthy additions to the foods we eat. Herbs are leaves while spices come from the seeds, flowers, bark and roots of plants. Different herbs and spices feature prominently in different cuisines around the world. Coriander, for example, is

particularly popular in Thai and Mexican cooking. Basil and oregano are often used in Italian recipes while paprika is a predominant spice in Spanish and Hungarian cuisine. Use more herbs and spices in your cooking for all the health benefits and the added flavour.

What is the main idea in the above text?

A Herbs and spices are used in different cuisines across the world.

B Herbs are leaves while spices come from the seeds, flowers, bark and roots of plants.

C Herbs and spices have a range of health benefits.

D Use more herbs and spices in your cooking for all the health benefits and the added flavour.

8 William plays two sports: tennis and AFL. Tennis involves training on Mondays and Wednesdays and playing in a competition on Saturday mornings. AFL training is on Tuesdays and Thursdays and games are on Saturday afternoons. On how many days during the period beginning on Wednesday 6 and ending after Sunday 24 did William play sport?

A 10

B 13

C 15

D 18

9 Jhulan says: 'Dirt is not soil. Dirt cannot grow plants. Dirt is dead. It cannot support life. Soil, on the other hand, contains minerals, nutrients, organic matter and living microscopic organisms, as well as insects and other animals such as worms. Soil supports life on Earth.'

Which one of these statements, if true, best supports Jhulan's claim?

A Healthy soil is vital to grow food.

B Dirt cannot support life.

C Farmers need to add nutrients to poor-quality soil.

D Poor agricultural practices deplete the soil.

10 A 4-by-5 grid is covered by two shapes as shown below. These shapes cannot be moved.

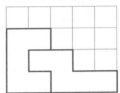

Which other two shapes **cannot** be used to cover the grid? The shapes may be rotated and reflected.

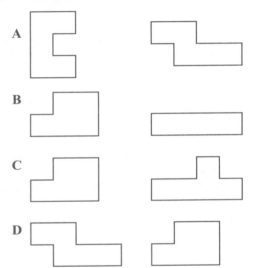

A

B

C

D

11 **Jeb**: 'I saw a poster in the window of Ray's Café. It says "Ray's Cafe—voted best coffee in the city". I wonder how many people voted and which coffee shops were included in the vote.'

If the information in the box is true, whose reasoning is **incorrect**?

Adriana: 'I'm sure all the city's cafes would need to have been involved in the competition otherwise Ray's couldn't state it was voted best in the city.'

Tevita: 'I've had coffee at Ray's and I think it makes the best coffee I've ever tasted because it's not bitter.'

Lulu: 'Only Ray's family members and friends would have been allowed to vote for Ray's to have been declared the best.'

Casey: 'I think customers should be told who was allowed to vote and how many other cafes were in the competition for Ray's Cafe to be able to say it was voted best coffee in the city.'

A Neither Casey nor Lulu

B Both Adriana and Casey

C Both Adriana and Lulu

D Neither Adriana nor Tevita

12 Which two dominoes from the five below will **not** complete the circuit of dominoes below?

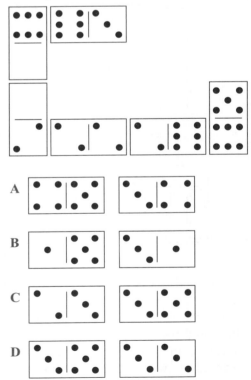

A

B

C

D

☞ Answers and explanations on pages 70–71

13 Emmeline's mother wrote a letter to the newspaper saying that Australians need to reduce the amount of food they waste.
She said the average household throws away 219 kilograms of food per year, which all goes to landfill.

Which one of these statements, if true, best supports Emmeline's mother's claim?

A Beef, bread, cheese and salad are the most thrown out foods in Australia.

B People should check what they already have in the fridge before they go shopping.

C A study found that an average of $965 per person per year is spent on wasted food.

D To cut down on bread wastage, freeze a loaf and only defrost slices as you need them.

14 A piece of square paper is folded along the diagonal to make a triangle. This triangle is folded in half along its line of symmetry to create another triangle. This triangle is folded in half three more times. The piece of paper is then unfolded and cut along the folds. How many small triangles are there?

A 64

B 32

C 16

D 8

15

Ms Brown runs the coding club. She says only those students who attended every club meeting last term will be allowed to enter this term's challenge.

Lucas: 'Oh no! I missed a club meeting last term so I won't be able to enter the challenge!'

Olivia: 'I attended every meeting last term so I'll definitely be entering the challenge.'

If the information in the box is true, whose reasoning is correct?

A Lucas only

B Olivia only

C Both Lucas and Olivia

D Neither Lucas nor Olivia

1 The award for the Most Improved in the 100-m sprint at a local athletics club goes to the athlete who has improved her personal best (PB) time the most since the beginning of the year.

At the beginning of the year the personal bests of the five U12 athletes were as follows:

Leila	21.5 s
Ashlyn	18.2 s
Tori	19.3 s
Akaya	16.8 s
Keisha	18.6 s

Their personal bests after one year of competition are shown here:

Leila	19.0 s
Ashlyn	16.4 s
Tori	16.5 s
Akaya	15.8 s
Keisha	17.1 s

Who won the award for Most Improved in the 100-m sprint?

A Leila   **B** Ashlyn   **C** Tori   **D** Akaya

2 In 2021 the United Kingdom became the first nation in the world to ban shark finning. Shark finning is where sharks are caught and have their fins cut off, sometimes while they are alive. The shark is then thrown back in the water where it slowly and painfully dies. Shark fins are sold to make shark-fin soup and some medicines. The ban on shark finning also means no shark-fin products can be imported to, exported from or sold in the UK. Shark finning is cruel, wasteful and bad for the marine ecosystem.

Which one of the following statements, if true, most **strengthens** the above argument?

A Sharks are essential species for a healthy marine environment.

B Shark finning is cruel, wasteful and bad for the marine ecosystem.

C The global shark population has been decimated by humans.

D Shark-fin soup is made using dried shark fins, chicken broth and herbs.

3 When making buttercream icing for a cake you need to leave the butter out of the fridge for a little while to soften slightly. Then it will beat smoothly with the sugar. The butter needs to still hold its shape so it can't be too soft. Test that the butter is at the right temperature for beating by pressing a finger on it. If your finger leaves an indent, the butter is ready to use. Don't leave it any longer or it might get too melted and not hold its shape.

If the information in the box is true, whose reasoning is **incorrect**?

A **Jett**: 'My icing was too runny. The butter must have melted too much.'

B **Tarna**: 'My butter and sugar did not beat easily. The butter must have been too hard.'

C **Jacqui**: 'I can't make a dent in my butter so I can't beat it with the sugar yet.'

D **Tao**: 'My icing was lumpy. I must have let it soften too much so it didn't beat smoothly.'

4 **Serena**: 'The speed limit for the stretch of McGregor Road between Smith St and Devon St must be reduced from 60 km per hour to 40 km per hour. That stretch of road is notorious for speeding. Three recent accidents involved vehicles travelling in excess of 90 km per hour.'

Which one of these statements, if true, most **weakens** Serena's argument?

A There is a bend in the road that is dangerous if taken at speed.

B Speeding is a risk factor for motor-vehicle accidents.

C The three accidents involved speeds in excess of 90 km per hour.

D There have only been three accidents related to excessive speed.

5 The dominoes are to be arranged in a square so that no number is placed next to itself.

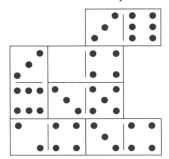

Which combination of two dominoes **cannot** be used to complete the square?

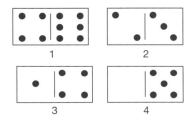

A 1 and 2

B 2 and 3

C 3 and 4

D 1 and 3

6 For the following question the top, front and right side of an object are the sides shown in the diagram below.

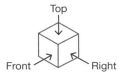

The top, front and right views of a 3D solid made from 10 cubes are shown below.

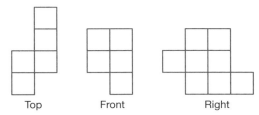

Which solid must it be?

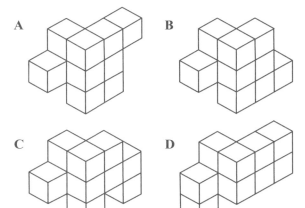

7 Five friends always sit on the same bench when waiting for the bus. There are only five spaces and no-one else uses the bus stop in the morning. Tahlia always sits next to Kyrie and Penny always sits next to Farrah. Jamal doesn't mind where he sits. Which of the following statements **cannot** be true?

A Tahlia sometimes sits next to Farrah.

B Tahlia never sits next to Penny.

C Jamal sometimes sits in the middle of the bench.

D Jamal sometimes sits in the second space from the left.

8 A bonsai is a tree that is pruned regularly so it stays very small. A bonsai is kept in a small, shallow plant pot. Even though a bonsai tree is small, it has the appearance of a mature tree.

Leah: 'Mum's friends from work are coming for dinner tonight. They asked if they could bring their dog Bonsai because it hates to be left at home alone.'

Josh: 'Bonsai must be a small dog like a Dachshund.'

Which assumption has Josh made?

A The dog's name is Bonsai.

B Only small dogs are named after small things.

C Bonsai must be a small dog.

D Only a small dog would hate to be left at home alone.

9 'Whoever moved Doug's canoe along the beach must have had an opportunity and a motive.'

If this is true, which one of these sentences must also be true?

A If Anita did not move the canoe, she cannot have had a motive.

B If Anita did not move the canoe, she cannot have had an opportunity.

C If Anita had both an opportunity and a motive, she must have moved the canoe.

D If Anita did not have a motive, she cannot have been the one to move the canoe.

10 Town A is south of Town B and east of Town D. Town C is south of Town A, north of Town E and west of Town F. Which town is south-east of Town A?

A Town C

B Town D

C Town E

D Town F

11 Ash is at Green Mall in the toy store.

Ash: 'I want to get my niece a toy for her birthday. Her dad told me she saw the one she wants in the window display at the Green Mall toy store but I can't seem to see it. My niece told her dad it's a purple dinosaur with yellow spots.'

Sales assistant: 'This dinosaur has yellow spots —it must be the one your niece wants!'

Which one of the following sentences shows the mistake the sales assistant has made?

A Ash's niece might now prefer a book about unicorns.

B Even if the toy is a dinosaur, it might not have yellow spots.

C There might be more than one toy dinosaur with yellow spots.

D Ash might be in the wrong store.

12 The local council surveyed some children to see what they would like included in a new playground. Hugo, Santi and Alex took part in the survey.

Hugo said he wanted an inground jumping pad, a curved slide, a climbing net, swings and a firefighter pole. Santi said she would like a large timber boat, a firefighter pole and swings. Alex wanted a curved slide, monkey bars, swings, a nature trail and a firefighter pole.

Based on the above information, what does Hugo want in a playground that neither Santi nor Alex wants?

A curved slide and inground jumping pad

B climbing net and swings

C inground jumping pad and climbing net

D nature trail and timber boat

13 Glenda signed up for an artist's retreat and must pick four workshops from the lists below. She must pick one from each list.

List 1	List 2	List 3	List 4
Sculpture	Knitting	Pencil sketching	Lino printing
Ceramics	Wood carving	Sculpture	Oil painting
Cross-stitch	Lino printing	Knitting	Ceramics
Oil painting	Charcoal drawing	Watercolour	Cross-stitch

If Glenda chooses Ceramics, Watercolour and Sculpture, what workshop can she **not** choose?

A Oil painting

B Lino printing

C Charcoal drawing

D Knitting

☞ **Answers and explanations on pages 72–73**

SAMPLE TEST 3A

14

David and his friends are catching the bus home from school.

David: 'We should sit near the door of the bus. It's faster to get off near the door.'

Which assumption has David made to draw his conclusion?

A Getting off the bus quickly will be a good thing.

B They should sit near the door of the bus.

C The bus is empty.

D It's faster to get off a bus if you sit near the door.

15 Kelly teaches drums to a number of students. She teaches every weekday afternoon except Friday and has a group session the last Sunday of each month. If the first of March falls on a Monday, how many days will she teach in all of March and April?

A 34

B 36

C 38

D 40

15 MIN

1 A fast train departed Paris on its way to Marseille at 7 am. It arrived at 12.30 pm. It departed for the return journey from Marseille to Paris one hour later. The train ran on time and took the same time to travel both legs of the trip.

At what time did it arrive back in Paris?

A 12.30 am

B 7 am

C 6.30 pm

D 7 pm

2 The first Metropolitan Traffic Act for Sydney, in 1902, set a speed limit of eight miles per hour (13 kilometres per hour) for the motor cars which had begun to appear on the roads since 1900. The speed limit was imposed on all roads within a 6-kilometre radius of the General Post Office in Martin Place in the heart of Sydney city. Councils outside of Sydney city were allowed to set their own speed limits and most set a limit between 10 and 16 kilometres per hour. By 1937 the speed limit in built-up areas had been gradually increased to 50 kilometres per hour, while 80 kilometres per hour was the limit on open roads.

Which one of these sentences can be concluded from the above information?

A Cars were allowed to travel faster in non–built up areas.

B The speed limit would have been increased over the years as cars became faster.

C The speed limit would have been increased when there were fewer horses on the roads.

D Councils outside of Sydney city would have had fewer pedestrians on the roads so could allow cars to go faster.

3 A sphere is placed on a hexagonal prism. Two views of the resulting solid are shown.

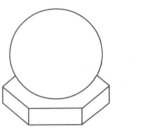 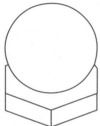

Which of the following **cannot** also be a view of the solid?

A 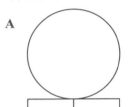 B

C 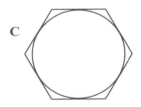 D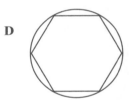

4 There is a community garden on Wattle Street. Tariq has a section of it where he grows carrots, pumpkins, silverbeet, beans and snow peas. Willem grows corn, zucchini, tomatoes, and iceberg and butter lettuces. Xia grows tomatoes, spring onions and corn, as well as iceberg, cos and butter lettuces.

Which vegetables does Xia grow that neither Tariq nor Willem grows?

A silverbeet and zucchini

B corn and spring onions

C tomatoes and snow peas

D spring onions and cos lettuces.

SAMPLE TEST 3B

5 Two green, two yellow and two blue beads are evenly spaced around a bracelet. The two greens are not next to each other.

What must also be the case?

A A yellow must be next to a blue.

B A green must be next to a blue.

C The two blues must be together.

D The greens must be directly opposite each other.

6 The following net is folded into a six-sided dice.

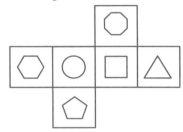

Which of the following is **not** a possible view of the dice?

A

B

C

D

7 **Maddie:** 'Whenever dad eats chocolate before bedtime, he finds it difficult to get to sleep. When he has too little sleep, he can't do his job effectively. And when he can't do his job effectively, he gets grumpy the next day and won't let us stay up to watch our favourite TV shows.'

Taane: 'We weren't allowed to stay up to watch TV on Tuesday night. Dad must have eaten chocolate before bedtime on Monday.'

Beth: 'If Dad eats chocolate tonight at bedtime, we are sure to miss out on staying up to watch our favourite TV shows tomorrow night.'

If the information in the box is true, whose reasoning is correct?

A Taane only

B Beth only

C Both Taane and Beth

D Neither Taane nor Beth

8 Three siblings are sitting across the back seat of a normal car. Anna has a window seat and Chris is sitting on Bella's left. Which of the following statements **cannot** be true?

A Chris is sitting in the left window seat.

B Bella is sitting in the left window seat.

C Bella is sitting in the right window seat.

D Chris is sitting in the middle seat.

9 Feral cats and domestic cats outside of the home kill billions of birds, amphibians, insects, reptiles and small mammals worldwide every year. They have contributed to the extinction of 63 species of animals. More must be done to protect wildlife from cats.

Which one of the following statements, if true, most **strengthens** the above argument?

A Cats have strong hunting instincts so a domestic cat, abandoned in the wild, quickly learns to fend for itself.

B True feral cats are cats that were born in the wild.

C In the wild, feral cats compete with native animals such as quolls and raptors for food and shelter.

D Feral cats are considered invasive pests in most parts of the world.

10 A 4-by-5 grid is covered by two shapes. They may be moved, rotated and reflected. For example, you could start with either of the following arrangements.

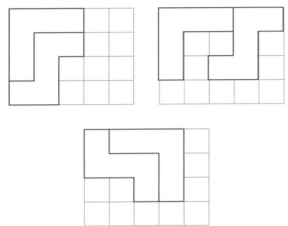

Which other two shapes **cannot** be used to cover the rest of the grid? The shapes may be rotated and reflected.

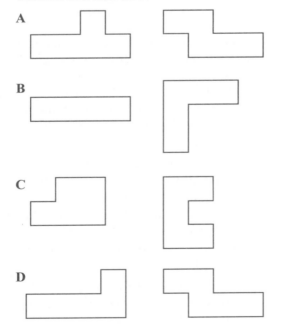

A

B

C

D

11 Divit's class was asked to vote on the topic for a whole-class debate. The topic choices were:

■ Every child should have a TV in their bedroom.
■ Every school day should begin with 20 minutes of exercise.
■ Does homework support learning?

Everyone had to cast two votes but they could not vote for the same topic twice. The topic would only be chosen if everyone voted for the same topic; if this did not happen, new topics would be chosen and the class would be asked to vote again. Every topic got at least one vote.

Knowing **one** of the following would allow us to know the result of the vote. Which one is it?

A Every student voted for either TV or homework, or both.

B No student voted for both exercise and TV.

C Exercise was one of the two more popular votes.

D Only four people voted for TV.

12 Helmut works casually at a restaurant. Between Tuesday 7 June and Thursday 30 June, he worked the dinner shift every Tuesday, Wednesday, Thursday and Saturday. He was ill on the 15th and did not work. How many shifts did he work in this period?

A 12   **B** 13
C 14   **D** 15

13 On Friday a small section of the school choir will be singing at a morning tea for some important visitors. Alice, Melia, Ben and Joe are in the choir. The choir teacher has just told them: 'If Alice does not sing on Friday, then Melia will sing. If Alice does sing, then Ben will sing in place of Joe.'

So, if Melia does not sing on Friday, which of the other three will sing?

A Alice only   **B** Alice and Ben
C Joe only   **D** Ben and Joe

SAMPLE TEST 3B

14 Tyree is exactly 800 m west of Gian in the bush. Tyree and Gian start walking at the same time. Tyree walks 200 m east, then 200 m north, 100 m east, 300 m south, then stops. Gian walks 300 m west, 100 m north, 100 m east, 200 m south, 100 m west, then stops.

How far are Tyree and Gian from each other now?

A 0 m
B 100 m
C 200 m
D 300 m

15 A robot nicknamed 'BeachBot' has been designed to clean up beach litter. This clever robot can drive around identifying different items it comes across. It can identify items that are litter and then pick them up. The designers also hope that BeachBot will make people more aware of the problem of litter on beaches and in oceans.

Which statement best expresses the main idea of the above text?

A BeachBot can detect different items of litter.
B Beach Bot uses Artificial Intelligence and image recognition to learn.
C The designers of BeachBot want to raise awareness about beach litter.
D Beachbot is a robot designed to clean up beach litter.

Answers and explanations on pages 73–75

SAMPLE TEST 4A

15 MIN

1 Three brands of paracetamol are sold at the chemist. Pain-Away is less expensive than Pain-Be-Gone and Bye-Pain is more expensive than Pain-Away. Which statement **must** be true?

A Bye-Pain is the most expensive brand.

B Pain-Away is the least expensive brand.

C Pain-Be-Gone is the most expensive brand.

D Pain-Be-Gone is the second most expensive brand.

2 Harriet and Nils were in the dog park. They heard a man calling for a dog. 'Brutus!' he called, loudly.

Nils: 'Brutus sounds like Brute. The dog must be big and scary.'

Which assumption has Nils made?

A Any dog with a big, scary-sounding name must be big and scary.

B Puppies grow up to look like the name they've been given.

C Dogs are named for their looks or behaviour.

D Some people like big, scary-looking dogs.

3 Two trains left Shanghai for Beijing at 5 pm. The high-speed train arrived in Beijing at 10 pm that same night. The slow train takes three times as long to complete the same journey. At what time will the slow train arrive in Beijing?

A 8 am

B 9 am

C 10.30 am

D 1 pm

4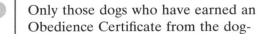
Only those dogs who have earned an Obedience Certificate from the dog-training school will be allowed to try out next week for work as security dogs.

Ellyse: 'Max's German Shepherd has an Obedience Certificate from the dog-training school so it will be given security work.'

Cody: 'Yumi's Border Collie does not have an Obedience Certificate from the dog-training school so it won't get any security work.'

If the information in the box is true, whose reasoning is correct?

A Ellyse only

B Cody only

C Both Ellyse and Cody

D Neither Ellyse nor Cody

5 Every year millions of tourists visit volcanoes around the world. They visit active, dormant and extinct volcanoes. There are more than 1500 active volcanoes in the world and 60 of them erupt every year. Volcano tourism is usually considered safe but volcanoes are intensely powerful and can be unpredictable so volcano tourism is not without risk.

Which one of these statements, if true, most **weakens** the above argument?

A In 2021 Iceland's Fagradalsfjall volcano erupted for the first time in nearly 800 years.

B Thousands of tourists travel each year to see the aftermath of an eruption.

C Extinct volcanoes are not expected to erupt anytime in the future.

D Volcanologists can usually predict if a volcano is about to erupt.

☞ **Answers and explanations on pages 75–77**

6 Toni and Francis leave from the same starting point on separate walks. Toni walks 100 m west, then 300 m north, 200 m east, 400 m south, then 200 m west. Francis walks 200 m north, 300 m west and then 300 m south.

Which option below best describes where they stand in relationship to each other now?

A Francis is 100 m west of Toni.

B Francis is 200 m east of Toni.

C Toni is 100 m west of Francis.

D Toni is 200 m east of Francis.

7 Six friends—Cristo, Mika, Brienne, Zilla, Rachel and Eloise—are seated around a rectangular table, so that one is at each end and two are on each side. Eloise is next to Mika and diagonally opposite Zilla. If Cristo is sitting directly opposite Mika and next to Rachel, who is sitting between Brienne and Cristo?

A Mika

B Rachel

C Zilla

D Eloise

8 There are 15 antechinus species native to Australia. An antechinus is a tiny Australian native mouse that is sometimes mistaken for a common non-native mouse but the two animals are different. Mice are rodents but the antechinus is a marsupial. Mice smell but antechinuses do not have any odour. Antechinuses have a longer narrower snout than a common mouse.

Based on the above information, whose reasoning is **incorrect**?

A **Ye**: 'A little marsupial mouse that doesn't smell bad sounds very cute.'

B **Antony**: 'The female antechinus must have a pouch for her babies.'

C **Piper**: 'The common mouse and the antechinus mouse are native to Australia.'

D **Viraj**: 'I think I'd be able to tell the difference between an antechinus and a common mouse if I looked at their noses.'

9 Working as a wildlife carer can be stressful but also rewarding. A female koala who had been badly burned in bushfires 18 months ago has been sighted in the wild with a joey on her back. The koala had spent 67 days recovering in a wildlife hospital before she could be released back into the wild. Carers were worried she would not survive and were thrilled to hear the good news that she has had a baby. Inspiring stories like these make the job of wildlife carer more rewarding.

Which of these sentences best expresses the main idea of the above text?

A A koala injured in a bushfire spent 67 days recovering in a wildlife hospital before she could be released back into the wild.

B Carers had feared for the koala's survival.

C Working as a wildlife carer can be stressful but also rewarding.

D A female koala who'd been badly burned in bushfires 18 months ago has been sighted in the wild with a joey on her back.

10 Kara had to choose four subjects to study. She must choose one subject from each list below.

List 1	List 2	List 3	List 4
Music	Sewing	Logic	Woodwork
English	English	Metals	Engineering
Computers	Woodwork	Sewing	Computers
Engineering	Metals	French	Music

Kara must choose English and wants to choose Engineering and Woodwork. Of the following options, which subject is Kara **definitely not** able to choose?

A French

B Computers

C Metals

D Sewing

11

Uma: 'I love cats! They are so cute. And they are fun to play with. My mum doesn't like them. But I sure do!'

Which statement best expresses Uma's main idea?

A Uma loves cats.

B Cats are cute.

C Uma's mum does not want a pet cat.

D Cats should be kept indoors.

12 Sajid's father is an author.

Lucia: 'Your father must have a good imagination!'

Which assumption has Lucia made to draw her conclusion?

A Sajid wants to be an author.

B Sajid's father has a good imagination.

C All authors have good imaginations.

D Sajid's father is an author.

13 As an elite swimmer, Kai usually trains twice each day on Mondays, Wednesdays and Fridays and once each day on Tuesdays, Thursdays and Saturdays. He has Sundays off. Kai went on holiday with his family from Wednesday 7th to Monday 19th of the same month. He began training again on Tuesday 20th. How many training sessions did he miss?

A 12

B 17

C 18

D 20

14 Jarrah's singing teacher told him: 'To have even a chance of passing the singing exam you must come to practice at least once a week for eight weeks.'

If Jarrah's singing teacher is correct, which of these statements must be true?

A All the students who come to practice at least once a week for eight weeks will pass the exam.

B Only the students who come to practice at least once a week for eight weeks will pass the exam.

C Some of the students who come to practice less than once a week for eight weeks will pass the exam.

D None of the students who come to practice less than once a week for eight weeks will pass the exam.

15 The diagram below shows five shapes arranged into a square.

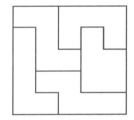

Which one of the following squares consists of the same five shapes as the diagram above? Shapes may be rotated or reflected.

A 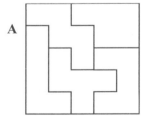   B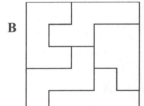

C 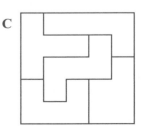   D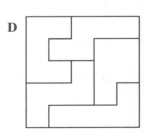

1 The two shapes below must be used with a third shape to cover the grid.

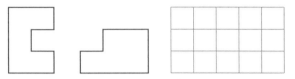

Which of the shapes below **cannot** be used? Shapes may be rotated and reflected.

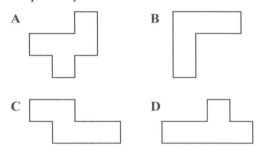

A   B

C   D

2 A sea lion walks on land on its large flippers. It has visible ear flaps. Seals have ear holes, no ear flaps and smaller flippers than sea lions which means they wriggle on land rather than walk.

Frankie: 'That seal-like sea mammal is scooting along on its belly. It doesn't seem to have ears. I think it's a seal.'

Rose: 'That other seal-like sea mammal seems to be trying to walk on its big flippers. And look, it has little furry ears—I think it's a sea lion.'

If the information in the box is true, whose reasoning is correct?

A Frankie only

B Rose only

C Both Frankie and Rose

D Neither Frankie nor Rose

3 Lauren usually goes to a gym session every weekday morning and once on Thursday evenings. If she goes away for work first thing on Tuesday 30 August and returns late Saturday 10 September, how many gym sessions has she missed?

A 10   **B** 11   **C** 12   **D** 13

4 Three friends collect stamps. Sometimes they trade them. Olivia has stamps to trade from France, Morocco, England, Scotland, Wales and Northern Ireland. Timothy has stamps to trade from Germany, Italy, Spain, Scotland, Portugal and France. Mira has stamps to trade from Germany, England, France, Spain, Italy, Poland, Morocco and Belgium.

Stamps from which countries does Olivia have that neither Timothy nor Mira has?

A Northern Ireland and Morocco

B Poland and Morocco

C Portugal and Scotland

D Northern Ireland and Wales

5 At a superhero movie marathon, ticket holders can choose to see four movies in a row from the timetable below. They must only choose one film from each session.

Session 1	Session 2	Session 3	Session 4
Avengers	Wonder Woman	Iron Man	Batman 2
Batman	Thor	Batman 2	Green Lantern
Iron Man	Green Lantern	Spiderman 2	Batman
Spiderman	Spiderman 2	Thor	Spiderman

Dimitri wants to see Spiderman and the two Batman films but he wants to see Batman before Batman 2. If he gets to see exactly what he wants, which movie will Dimitri be unable to see at the movie marathon?

A Iron Man

B Wonder Woman

C Spiderman 2

D Green Lantern

6 Nine balls, numbered 1 to 9, are spread out on a pool table. Helen strikes the 5-ball which hits another ball. This ball then strikes the 8-ball, which is sunk in a pocket.

Which of the following statements must be true?

A The second ball showed a higher number than 5.

B No ball struck another ball with a lower number on it.

C At least one ball struck a ball with a higher number on it.

D The second ball showed a lower number than 8.

7

Zane: 'It's Mum's birthday on Sunday. Her favourite colour is black. She loves black clothes and she wears nail polish so I'll buy her black nail polish for her birthday. '

Which assumption has Zane made?

A Because black is Mum's favourite colour she will like black clothes.

B It's Mum's birthday so Zane needs to buy a gift.

C Mum will like black nail polish.

D Mum likes Zane to buy gifts rather than make them.

8 One of five envelopes contains the code to a safe. The envelopes are arranged in a row. The white envelope is two spaces from the grey one, which is in the middle of the row. The blue envelope is two spaces from the pink one and is next to the red one. If the code is in the envelope next to the white envelope, in which envelope is it?

A red   **B** grey

C blue   **D** pink

9 Butterflies help pollinate flowers so they are essential for agricultural crops as well as wildflowers. Ninety per cent of plants need pollinators such as butterflies. Without pollinators, plants would not be able to reproduce. Butterflies are also essential to the survival of animals that eat butterflies. Without butterflies entire ecosystems could collapse.

Which of these statements, if true, most **strengthens** the above argument?

A Organic farming, which does not use pesticides, increases the survival rate of butterflies.

B Butterflies need grasslands, flowers, pastures, meadows and uncultivated margins of fields.

C Nearly two thirds of invertebrates need butterflies in the food chain to survive.

D Butterflies live on every continent in the world except Antarctica.

10 Seven cubes are attached to create the solid below.

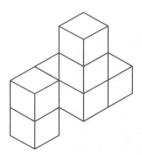

Which is **not** a possible view of the solid?

A   **B**

C   **D**

11

Mr Thomas: 'Children in a class of 27 were told to wear red, blue or yellow to school today for team games. I saw 20 children this morning wearing their team colours. The other seven, not in team colours, must have brought clothes to change into at school.'

Which one of these sentences shows the mistake Mr Thomas has made?

A He did not include the children from other classes.

B He did not say which children must have brought clothes to change into.

C He did not realise some of the children who wore coloured clothing might have worn the wrong colour.

D He did not realise some of the children might not have remembered to bring coloured clothing.

12 There are five towns in a rural area. Town A is north-west of Town C. Town D is south-east of Town B. Town B is due north of Town E and Town D is due east of Town C.

Which of the following **cannot** be a map of the area?

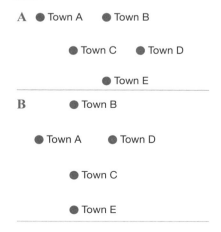

A ● Town A   ● Town B

      ● Town C   ● Town D

          ● Town E

B   ● Town B

  ● Town A   ● Town D

     ● Town C

     ● Town E

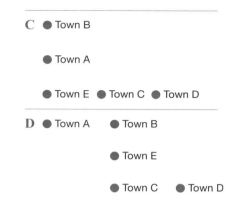

C ● Town B

   ● Town A

   ● Town E ● Town C ● Town D

D ● Town A   ● Town B

      ● Town E

    ● Town C   ● Town D

13

Only those students who hand in their permission notes by tomorrow will be allowed to go on the excursion to the rock pools next week.'

Ella: 'I've already handed in my permission note so I'll definitely be able to go on the excursion.'

Anh: 'Oh no! I forgot to bring my note back today so I won't be able to go on the excursion.'

If the information in the box is true, whose reasoning is correct?

A Ella only

B Anh only

C Both Ella and Anh

D Neither Ella nor Anh

14 Three runners are in three lanes of an athletics track. Usain is inside Asafa and Asafa is outside Donovan.

Which of the following statements **cannot** be true?

A Asafa is between Usain and Donovan.

B Donovan is in the inside lane.

C Usain is in the inside lane.

D Donovan is between Asafa and Usain.

15

Harry: 'I've got a banana for lunch again today!'

Katy: 'You must really like bananas!'

Which assumption has Katy made to draw her conclusion?

A Anyone who has a banana for lunch two days running must really like bananas.

B Harry really likes bananas.

C Harry has had a banana for lunch two days running.

D Harry's father packed his lunchbox and Harry does not like bananas.

15 MIN

1 The shape shown is one of five that must be used to cover the grid below.

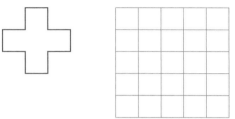

To cover the rest of the grid, you must use four of the exact same shape. For which shape is this possible? Shapes may be rotated and reflected.

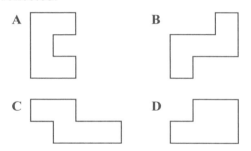

2 A drummer is a percussionist but a percussionist is not necessarily a drummer.

A drummer plays on a drum kit. A percussionist plays any number of different percussion instruments including timpani, cymbals, gongs, drums, tambourines, maracas and chimes. A drummer uses drum sticks. A percussionist usually just uses their hands.

Whose reasoning is flawed?

A **Harry**: 'Samar is a percussionist who does not play the drums.'

B **Kelly**: 'Zi is the drummer in a band called Cloud. He sometimes plays the tambourine too.'

C **Brooke:** 'Jeremy plays drums, cymbals, gongs, timpani, and chimes. He's a percussionist who never uses drum sticks.'

D **Arya**: 'Raina only plays the drums and no other instruments so she's a drummer and not a percussionist.'

3 John is speaking to co-workers in an office environment. John says: 'I know some of you find it hard to work effectively in the heat. I also know many people worry about the cost of air conditioning on our power bills as well as the cost to the planet of using so much electricity so let's have a vote. You have two votes each but you cannot vote for the same option twice. We will only implement an option if everyone votes for it; otherwise I won't turn on anything.'

You can vote as follows:

1 Turn on the fan only.

2 Turn on the air conditioning only.

3 Turn on both the fan and the air conditioning.

If every option got at least one vote, knowing **one** of the following would allow us to know the result of the vote. Which one is it?

A Everyone voted for either the fan only or the air conditioning only.

B No-one voted for both the fan and the air conditioning, and the air conditioning only.

C Air conditioning only was the most popular vote.

D Only two people voted for the fan only.

4 The back row of an old team photo consisted of four friends. Looking at the photo, Grant was further left than Malcolm, and Terry was immediately to the right of Jim. Given this limited information, who is definitely not standing in the third spot from the left?

A Grant

B Malcolm

C Terry

D Jim

5 A dietician has suggested that healthy eating is an important aspect of children's education and that children should spend more time in school learning how to cook healthy food.

Which one of these statements, if true, best supports the dietician's claim?

A Learning how to cook improves children's understanding of healthy eating.

B Some children don't know whether foods are healthy or unhealthy.

C Some children hope to become celebrity chefs.

D Cooking has been taught in schools in the past.

6 The following net is folded into a six-sided dice.

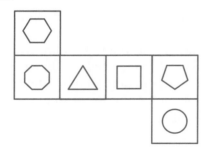

Which of the following is **not** a possible view of the dice?

A 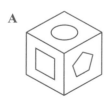　　B

C 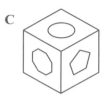　　D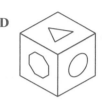

7 Seven cubes are attached to create the solid below.

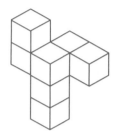

Which is **not** a possible view of the solid?

A 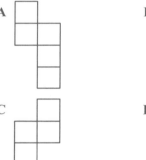　　B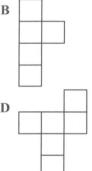

C　　D

8

Erica: 'Blake must hate doing homework because he never does it.'

What assumption has Erica made?

A Blake does not understand the homework.

B Blake's parents don't help him with his homework.

C People don't do things they hate doing.

D Blake's parents need him to do other things at home after school.

9 Fossil remains of a dinosaur suggest the type of food the dinosaur ate. Like all toothed animals, dinosaurs had teeth suited to their diet. Most dinosaurs were herbivores. Herbivorous dinosaurs had beaks or flat teeth that they used to snip, strip or grind vegetation. Carnivorous dinosaurs had sharp teeth for ripping flesh. Omnivore dinosaurs sometimes had a mixture of teeth.

Which of the following statements is the main idea of the above text?

A Most dinosaurs were herbivores.

B Scientists like to examine dinosaur fossils.

C Carnivorous dinosaurs had sharp teeth for ripping flesh.

D Fossil remains of a dinosaur suggest the type of food the dinosaur ate.

10 Before setting off on a long hiking trip, Fatma must choose four courses she would like to do in preparation. The timetable for the activities is below.

Session 1	Session 2	Session 3	Session 4
Map reading	Tent construction	Morse code	First aid
Fire building	First aid	Finding water	Orienteering
Finding water	Abseiling	Map reading	Fire building
Morse code	Fire building	First aid	Abseiling

Fatma wants to choose Fire building, Morse code and Map reading. Which other course will she be unable to choose?

A Abseiling

B Orienteering

C First aid

D Finding water

11 Terry and Nina are in the playground before school.

Nina: 'Let's practise soccer kicks.'

Terry: 'We'd better not break any windows. Mr Small will be angry if we do!'

Which assumption has Terry made to draw his conclusion?

A They had better not break any windows.

B Nina is the best player on the team.

C Mr Small will be angry if they break a window.

D They must not do anything to make Mr Small angry.

12 Gemma's father wants to learn how to knit. He says: 'I'm going to try to knit a scarf. It will be easier than knitting a blanket.'

Which one of these statements, if true, most **weakens** Gemma's father's claim?

A Gemma's father likes to try new things.

B Gemma's father has chosen a pattern that is very complicated.

C A scarf is much smaller than a blanket.

D Gemma's father does not like wearing scarves.

13 Chantelle sets herself a challenge to go on a bike ride every Wednesday and Saturday in September and October this year. If the first of September is a Thursday, how many rides will she go on?

A 13

B 15

C 17

D 19

14

A cumquat is an orange fruit. It can be round or oval shaped. It is smaller than a mandarin.

Mira: 'The fruit on that tree is orange and round. It might be a mandarin tree.'

Lee: 'But the fruit is very small. It could be a cumquat tree.'

If the information in the box is true, whose reasoning is correct?

A Mira only

B Lee only

C Both Mira and Lee

D Neither Mira nor Lee

15 At a birthday party, Kareem must choose to open one of five different-shaped boxes that are lined up in a row. There is a square box, a circular box, a triangular box, a hexagonal box and a rectangular box. There is a vanilla cake in one box, a chocolate cake in another and a cheesecake in a third. The other two boxes are empty.

- The circular box is next to the triangular box.
- The rectangular box is four spaces from the square and three spaces from the circular box.
- The chocolate cake is in a box next to the circular box.
- The vanilla cake is three spaces from the chocolate cake.
- The cheesecake is not between the vanilla and the chocolate.

Kareem opens the hexagonal box. What does he find inside?

A an empty box

B chocolate cake

C cheesecake

D vanilla cake

☞ **Answers and explanations on pages 78–80**

15 MIN

1 Bonnie, Zak, Ash and Mitch live in the only four houses in a row on the same side of their street. The street runs from east to west. Bonnie lives east of Zak, Mitch lives west of Ash and Bonnie lives east of Mitch. Who **cannot** live in the second house to the east?

A Bonnie

B Zak

C Ash

D Mitch

2 Riku stores his lunch in the communal fridge at his workplace. On Friday someone had taken his lunch before he'd had time to eat it. Whoever took Riku's lunch must have had both an opportunity and a motive.

If this is true, which one of these sentences **cannot** be true?

A Whoever took the lunch must have had a motive.

B If someone did not take the lunch, they cannot have had an opportunity.

C If someone did not have a motive, they cannot have been the one to take the lunch.

D If someone did not have an opportunity, they must have been the one to take it.

3 Gordon went to a cooking course, where he could learn to cook many different cuisines. He had to pick a cuisine for each session listed below.

Session 1	Session 2	Session 3	Session 4
Italian	Japanese	German	Vietnamese
Chinese	Vietnamese	Lebanese	Italian
Thai	Chinese	Moroccan	French
German	French	Thai	Japanese

Gordon chooses Vietnamese, German and Moroccan. Which of the following did Gordon **definitely not** choose as his fourth cuisine?

A Japanese

B Chinese

C Thai

D Italian

4 Three friends discussed the countries they want to travel to. Ronald said he wanted to travel to the Philippines, Hawaii, Tahiti, Japan, Vietnam and Cambodia. Doris plans to travel to Japan, China, South Korea, Thailand, Vietnam and Fiji. Carl wants to travel to Hawaii, Noumea, Fiji, Tahiti, New Zealand and Japan.

Which countries does Ronald want to visit that neither Carl nor Doris wants to visit?

A Vietnam and Tahiti

B the Philippines and New Zealand

C Noumea and Cambodia

D the Philippines and Cambodia

5 Animesh and Perry both competed in the 800-m running race. Animesh runs 75 metres in the same time it takes Perry to run 80 metres. When Perry finishes the race, how many metres does Animesh still have to go?

A 10 metres

B 25 metres

C 50 metres

D 80 metres

6 Jenna has athletics training every Tuesday, Wednesday and Thursday. In one particular month she didn't miss a session and trained exactly 13 times. If the first of the month was a Tuesday, how many days were in the month?

A 28   **B** 29   **C** 30   **D** 31

7 Bradley said: 'I'm selling my old phone. It's a good phone and there's nothing wrong with it.'

Which one of these statements, if true, best supports Bradley's ability to sell his phone?

A The phone is in excellent condition.

B The phone is only three years old.

C I got a new phone for my birthday so I don't need the old one anymore.

D If I can't sell it, I'll give it away or recycle it.

8 Eels have an amazing migration story. They deserve our respect and admiration. Tiny transparent baby eels, born in the Coral Sea off North Queensland, float south on ocean currents, not eating at all until they reach the mouth of a river where they become darker in colour and become known as elver. They swim up rivers and can even travel across dry land, breathing oxygen through their skin, in their quest for a body of inland water to call home. They stay in this waterway and grow into adults. When it is time to breed they head back the way they came, down the river and out to sea. Researchers have found that adult eels can swim over 2600 kilometres from inland dams and rivers back to the Coral Sea where they were born so they can breed. What an amazing animal the eel is!

Which of the following statements best expresses the main idea of the text?

A Eels travel from the sea and back to the sea.

B Eels have an amazing migration story.

C What an amazing animal the eel is!

D Researchers have found that adult eels can swim over 2600 kilometres back to sea.

9 Seven cubes are attached to create the solid below.

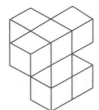

Which is **not** a possible view of the solid?

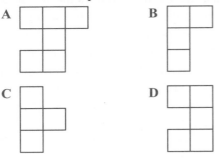

10 Hawks and eagles are birds of prey. An eagle has a longer wingspan than a hawk and eagles tend to be larger and more powerful than hawks. Most eagles have feathers down to their toes. Both types of birds eat insects, smaller birds and small mammals. Eagles also eat fish.

Lenny: 'That bird is big and strong looking with long wings. It must be an eagle and not a hawk.'

Jennifer: 'But that bird is eating a mouse. It can't be an eagle.'

If the information in the box is true, whose reasoning is **incorrect**?

A Lenny only

B Jennifer only

C Both Lenny and Jennifer

D Neither Lenny nor Jennifer

11 A dog trainer has suggested that dogs should not be fed food from a bowl. Instead an owner should play training games with their dog and use the dog's daily food allowance as rewards.

Which one of these statements, if true, best supports the dog trainer's claim?

A Playing games with your dog increases the dog's confidence.

B Most dogs do not like having a bone taken away from them.

C If you feed from a bowl, keep the tastiest food as treats.

D Feeding away from the bowl promotes a dog's mental and physical enrichment.

12 The following is a view of a six-sided dice.

Which of the following is **not** a possible net of the dice?

A

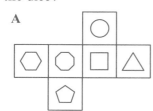

B

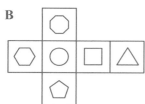

C

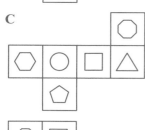

D

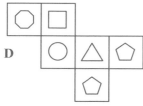

13 The diagram below shows five shapes arranged into a square.

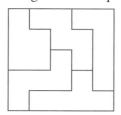

Which one of the following squares consist of the same five shapes as the diagram above? Shapes may be rotated or reflected.

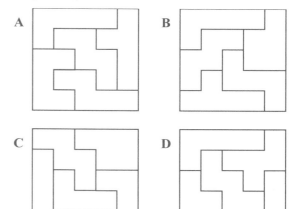

14 The ace, king, queen and jack of hearts are placed on a table. The ace, king and queen are face up and the jack is face down. A move is said to have been made when two cards are flipped over.

After one move, what is **not** a possible view of the cards?

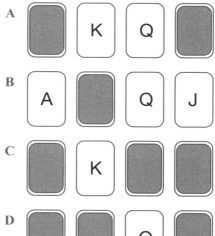

15

The 'abandon ship' signal on a cruise ship is seven short blasts followed by one long blast on the general alarm and then on the ship's whistle. When it sounds, it could either be a drill or it could be a real emergency call to abandon ship. Abandon ship drills happen once a week, always at exactly three o'clock in the afternoon. But they can happen on any day.'

Liora: 'If the 'abandon ship' signal has not sounded, it doesn't mean there isn't an emergency.'

James: 'You know it must be a real 'abandon ship' signal if you hear it in the middle of the night!'

If the information in the box is true, whose reasoning is correct?

A Liora only

B James only

C Both Liora and James

D Neither Liora nor James

☞ **Answers and explanations on pages 80–81**

IDENTIFYING THE MAIN IDEA Page 1

1   **C is correct.** The main idea is that Moira Newi was the first Indigenous woman to receive a medal for heroic conduct. C is the option that best expresses this. The rest of the text gives additional information about who Moira was and what she did that was heroic.

A and B are incorrect. This is supporting information for the main idea.

D is incorrect. This information is not in the text so cannot be the main idea.

2   **D is correct.** The aim of the 100 Year Starship project is for humans to travel to other stars. This is mentioned in the opening sentence and reinforced in the conclusion. The rest of the text gives additional information about the project.

A and C are incorrect. This is supporting information for the main idea.

B is incorrect. This information is not in the text so cannot be the main idea. The text tells us the aim is to be able to build a starship in 100 years time, not that a starship takes 100 years to build.

IDENTIFYING A CONCLUSION THAT MUST BE TRUE Page 2

1   **C is correct.** According to the instructor if an applicant has not already made at least five films, then they do not have a chance of being accepted into the workshop. Therefore none of the applicants who have made less than five films will be accepted into the workshop—so this statement must be true.

A is incorrect. According to the instructor, having already made five films gives an applicant only a **chance** of being accepted. It does not guarantee acceptance.

B is incorrect. The instructor says applicants must have made at least five films, not less than five films.

D is incorrect. The instructor says applicants must have made at least five films so this statement cannot be true.

2   **B is correct.** Vultures and snakes are both included in the list of animals Emma would like to see but neither Hank nor Ilya mentions either of these animals.

A is incorrect. Emma wants to see the condors and vultures but Ilya would also like to see the condors.

C is incorrect. Emma wants to see snakes and meerkats but both Hank and Ilya would also like to see meerkats.

D is incorrect. Emma doesn't want to see the platypuses or giraffes.

IDENTIFYING A CONCLUSION THAT IS NOT POSSIBLE Page 3

1   **A is correct.** The store that gave customers $100 worth of groceries for every fridge purchased charges $50 for delivery so it cannot be true that Ashleigh got free delivery.

B is incorrect. This option could be true. Ashlee wants a new fridge but she might not buy one.

C is incorrect. It is possible that Ashlee purchased a fridge and got it delivered for free from the store that was not offering a free portable cooler.

D is incorrect. It could be true that Ashlee purchased a fridge from the third store and got it delivered for free.

2   **B is correct.** It is not possible for Henry to improve his playing if he only practises on Wednesdays for two hours. You are told he needs to practise at least twice a week for an hour each time but the second hour of his current two-hour practice session doesn't help him improve because he is too tired.

A is incorrect. It is possible that Henry will not improve if he continues practising only on Wednesdays for two hours.

C is incorrect. It is possible that Henry will not improve if he only practises for one hour on a Wednesday.

D is incorrect. It is possible that Henry will give up playing the violin, especially if he doesn't have the time or the inclination to continue practising.

IDENTIFYING **EVIDENCE THAT LEADS TO A CONCLUSION** Page 4

1 **D is correct.** Jamie will not be able to make a chocolate cake if one of Harold's best friends is allergic to chocolate, even though that is one of Harold's favourite types of cake. You should also conclude that Jamie won't make a sponge cake if that is Harold's least favourite cake. Therefore you can draw the conclusion that Jamie most likely made a banana cake. The statement that one of the friends doesn't particularly like the taste of bananas is not as significant a reason to judge that Jamie won't choose to make banana cake rather than a chocolate or sponge cake.

2 **D is correct.** Because every student had two votes, knowing that no student voted for both dressing up as a monster or not dressing up at all tells you all students must have voted for book characters with one of their votes. Knowing the other options doesn't allow you to know the result of the vote.

 A is incorrect. This only lets you know that the result was either not dressing up at all or book characters.

 B is incorrect. This only lets you know that not dressing up did not win.

 C is incorrect. This only lets you know that monsters could have won but not that it did win.

IDENTIFYING **AN ASSUMPTION** Page 5

1 **C is correct.** For the conclusion to hold it must be assumed that everyone likes kittens. (The pet store has cute kittens for sale + everyone likes kittens means therefore everyone will want a kitten.)

 A is incorrect. This is the purpose of the advertisement.

 B is incorrect. This is the evidence the writer has used to support this conclusion.

 D is incorrect. This is the conclusion the writer has drawn, based on the assumption that everyone likes kittens.

2 **A is correct.** Aziz's conclusion is that Bruno is a good soccer player. He has based this conclusion on the evidence that Bruno scored a goal. So for his conclusion to hold it must be assumed that anyone who scores a goal is a good soccer player. (Bruno scored a goal at soccer on Saturday + anyone who scores a goal is a good soccer player means therefore Bruno is a good soccer player.)

 B is incorrect. This would not support the conclusion that Bruno is a good soccer player.

 C is incorrect. This is Aziz's conclusion.

 D is incorrect. This is the evidence Aziz has used to draw his conclusion.

IDENTIFYING **CORRECT REASONING** Page 6

1 **A is correct.** The information tells you students must have completed their workbook pages satisfactorily to be allowed to play indoor games after lunch. Martin has not done this so Joshi's reasoning is correct.

 B is incorrect. Ella is incorrect to state that Vivian will be allowed to play indoor games after lunch because, although she says Vivian has completed her workbook pages, she cannot know whether or not Vivian's work is satisfactory.

 C is incorrect. Ella is not correct so this option is incorrect.

 D is incorrect. Joshi's reasoning is correct so this option is incorrect.

2 **B is correct.** Benedict uses correct reasoning when he states that if the petrol icon is not orange or red, there's no need to refuel urgently.

 A is incorrect. The information in the box tells you the petrol light only lights up when the tank is starting to run low on fuel or there's only enough fuel for ten kilometres of travel. It doesn't show any light when the tank is full.

 C is incorrect. The orange light tells you that you are starting to run low on fuel. The orange light does not indicate you have run out of fuel so Mei's reasoning is incorrect.

D is incorrect. Peter is incorrect to state that if the petrol light flashes red, you need to find a petrol station within twenty kilometres. The information tells you to refuel within ten kilometres of travel.

IDENTIFYING FLAWED REASONING
Page 8

1 **A is correct.** Vanessa's reasoning is incorrect. She can't know for certain that Jing must have left the cake in the oven too long. She has not allowed for the possibility of the cake being dry for other reasons.

   B is incorrect. The reasoning used is correct. Ed says Jing **might** not have measured exactly. This is a less certain response than Vanessa's and allows for other reasons to be correct.

   C is incorrect. The reasoning used is correct. Ollie says **maybe** he used less sugar. This is a less certain response than Vanessa's and allows for other reasons to be correct.

   D is incorrect. The reasoning used is correct. Amy says it's **possible** that Jing overbaked the cake. This is a less certain response than Vanessa's and allows for other reasons to be correct.

2 **D is correct.** There could be more than one brand of soy milk that uses blue and white on the carton. Dom cannot claim with certainty that he has found the soy milk Gran asked for just because he has found one in a blue-and-white carton.

   A is incorrect. It is irrelevant whether or not Dom likes soy milk.

   B is incorrect. Gran might not like the soy milk Dom has found—if he hasn't found the correct one—but this isn't the mistake Dom has made.

   C is incorrect. It might be possible that Dom has found the correct soy milk but his mistake is that he stated it **definitely was** the milk Gran wanted.

IDENTIFYING ADDITIONAL EVIDENCE TO STRENGTHEN A CLAIM
Page 9

1 **D is correct.** The politician claims that floods are good for agriculture. The refilling of aquifers and farm dams would be of benefit to a farm so it supports this claim.

A and C are incorrect. These statements do not support the politician's claim; rather they weaken it.

B is incorrect. This statement is not relevant to the claim that floods are good for agriculture.

2 **B is correct.** This statement shows how extreme the habitat loss is and gives further evidence to support it.

   A is incorrect. The environmentalist's claim is that Australian species are facing extreme habitat loss. The statement that scientists are conducting wildlife surveys does not best support this, although the findings of those surveys might.

   C is incorrect. This statement does not support the claim about extreme habitat loss.

   D is incorrect. This could be part of the solution to the problem of habitat loss claimed by the environmentalist. However, it does not best support the claim that Australian species are facing extreme habitat loss.

IDENTIFYING ADDITIONAL EVIDENCE TO WEAKEN AN ARGUMENT
Page 10

1 **B is correct.** The statement that most people struggle to manage hooping effectively weakens the claim that hooping is great fun. Generally people might think that struggling to manage the hula hoop will not be fun.

   A is incorrect. This statement provides additional evidence that hooping is popular around the world and good for fitness so it strengthens the claim that hooping is fun and develops fitness.

   C and D are incorrect. These statements provide additional information about hooping but do not weaken the claim.

2 **C is correct.** Archie says he doesn't like driving in the rain and because the Bureau of Meteorology has predicted it might rain on Friday, he suggests not driving to Old Pa's. The statement that weakens Archie's argument is that the Bureau of Meteorology has only said it **might** rain on Friday, not that it **definitely will** rain all day on Friday.

A is incorrect. This statement is a reason to drive to see Old Pa on Friday. It strengthens the need to get to Old Pa's on Friday. It doesn't weaken Archie's claim about driving in the rain.

B is incorrect. This statement is a reason to drive to see Old Pa on Friday but it doesn't weaken Archie's claim about the rain.

D is incorrect. The statement that the Bureau of Meteorology is very accurate with its predictions somewhat strengthens Archie's claim. It doesn't weaken Archie's claim that they'd better not drive because of the rain.

ANSWERING QUESTIONS ABOUT DIFFERENCES IN TRAVEL TIMES
Page 11

1   **B is correct.** It will take 2 hours 30 minutes.

You need to find out how much faster the high-speed train is than the slow train so work out how many times the fast train could do its trip in 3 hours, i.e. 3 hours divided by 45 minutes.

$$3 \text{ hours} = 180 \text{ minutes}$$
$$180 \text{ minutes} \div 45 \text{ minutes} = 4$$

The high-speed train is four times faster than the slow train.

So a high-speed trip between Sydney and Melbourne will take a quarter of the time it takes the slow train to make it.

10 hours ÷ 4 = 2.5 hours = 2 hours 30 minutes

2   **C is correct.** Jeremy arrives back at 7.20 am.

If Jeremy runs three times faster than he walks, it will take him three times as long to walk as to run the same distance. $3 \times 20 = 60$ minutes. It will take him 60 minutes (1 hour) to walk home from the harbour. After running for 20 minutes then walking for 60 minutes he arrives home 80 minutes (1 hour 20 minutes) after 6 am, which is 7.20 am.

Decimal (hours)	Fraction (hours)	Minutes
0.1	$\frac{1}{10}$	6
0.2	$\frac{1}{5}$	12
0.25	$\frac{1}{4}$	15
0.3	$\frac{3}{10}$	18
0.333 3333	$\frac{1}{3}$	20
0.4	$\frac{2}{5}$	24
0.5	$\frac{1}{2}$	30
0.6	$\frac{3}{5}$	36
0.666 6666	$\frac{2}{3}$	40
0.7	$\frac{7}{10}$	42
0.75	$\frac{3}{4}$	45
0.8	$\frac{4}{5}$	48
0.9	$\frac{9}{10}$	54
1	1	60

SELECTING ITEMS FROM A NUMBER OF LISTS
Page 12

1   **D is correct.** Ben cannot choose non-fiction.

Biographies is only available in session 2 so Ben must choose Biographies from session 2. Graphic Novels can then only be chosen from session 4 and Crime from session 1. This means Ben's fourth choice must be from session 3. Non-fiction is not available in session 3 so cannot be chosen.

2   **C is correct.** Celia cannot choose Lauren Jackson.

Jessica Fox can only be heard during session 3. That means Steve Waugh must be chosen from session 2. Patty Mills can be chosen from either session 1 or session 4. This means any sportsperson in session 1 or 4 can be chosen. Lauren Jackson only appears in session 2 when Celia is listening to Steve Waugh and session 3 when Celia is listening to Jessica Fox. So Celia cannot also hear Lauren Jackson speak.

DECIDING HOW MANY DAYS OR EVENTS LIE BETWEEN SPECIFIC DATES
Page 13

1 D is correct. Virat will play cricket 18 times in January.

January has 31 days. That is four full weeks plus three extra days. If the month starts on a Saturday, the three extra days will be Saturday 29, Sunday 30 and Monday 31. Virat will play on the Saturday and Monday. The total number of games is given by:

4 weeks × 4 sessions + 2 extra sessions
= 16 + 2 = 18

2 C is correct. There will be 29 performances.

Between Wednesday 23 and Saturday 17 there are three full weeks and four extra days. The four extra days are Wednesday to Saturday. In a full week the orchestra plays eight shows: one every day except for Monday and an extra show on both Saturday and Sunday. From Wednesday to Saturday the orchestra plays five shows: one each day and a second show on Saturday. The total number of shows is given by:

3 weeks × 8 shows + 5 extra shows = 29 shows

You can see this in the calendar below. The circled are days with two performances.

November

Su	M	Tu	W	Th	F	Sa
30	31	1	2	3	4	5
6	7	8	9	10	11	12
13	14	15	16	17	18	19
20	21	22	23	24	25	㉖
㉗	28	29	30	1	2	3

December

Su	M	Tu	W	Th	F	Sa
27	28	29	30	1	2	③
④	5	6	7	8	9	⑩
⑪	12	13	14	15	16	⑰
18	19	20	21	22	23	24
25	26	27	28	29	30	31

ARRANGING SHAPES SO THEY FIT TOGETHER
Page 14

1 A is correct.

Here is the solution for A. There are no solutions for the other answers.

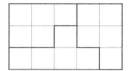

2 C is correct.

Here are the solutions for the other options. There is no solution for C.

ANSWERING QUESTIONS INVOLVING THE DIRECTIONS ON A COMPASS
Page 16

1 D is correct. Ealing is the furthest east. Chester is south-east of Derby but south-west of Ealing. This means Ealing is furthest east of the three. Derby is north-east of Albany so Albany (and Boothby) must be to the west of Derby. So Ealing is also further east than Albany. A possible diagram of the area is given.

2 D is correct. Town C must be directly north of Town B. In diagram D it is not.

ANSWERING QUESTIONS INVOLVING DIFFERENT VIEWS OF THE SAME OBJECT
Page 18

1 D is correct.

B is incorrect. It has five rooms.

A is incorrect. No single room extends all the way down the long side of the building. Every room shares at least one wall with the outside of the building.

C is incorrect. Its middle room is surrounded by other rooms.

2 C is correct.

A is the view from front right. B is the view from back right. D is the view from the top. C is not a view of the solid.

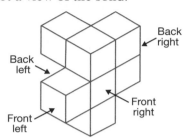

Note that the question specifies 7 cubes. This means there is not a cube hidden behind the ones visible as all 7 are visible.

ORDERING ITEMS IN A ROW OR AROUND A TABLE
Page 20

1 C is correct. Box D contains the prize.

Once boxes B and E are placed at the ends of the row, we can see that Box C must be in the middle of the row as it is two spaces from Box E. This means boxes A and D must occupy the remaining positions and Box D is the only box that is two spaces from A so it must contain the prize.

$$B - A - C - D - E$$
$$B - D - C - A - E$$

2 A is correct. The blue bead is next to a red bead.

Once the green and yellow beads have been placed so that the green is not next to a yellow and the yellows are not next to each other, the bracelet looks like this:

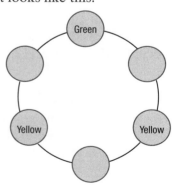

The other beads can be placed in any arrangement. We can see that the blue bead can be placed next to the green or opposite the green, which is also between the two yellows. It can never be next to a red bead.

ANSWERING QUESTIONS WITH NETS, DICE AND DOMINOES
Page 21

1 D is correct. From the net we can work out that the pentagon and the hexagon should be on opposite sides of the dice. This is because they are in a row and separated by another face (the circle). In D they are next to each other. So D cannot be created from the net.

2 D is correct. The minimum roll would be two circles ($1 \times 1 = 1$) and the maximum would be two octagons ($8 \times 8 = 64$). The difference is $64 - 1 = 63$.

IDENTIFYING WHAT IS TRUE OR WHAT CANNOT BE TRUE WHEN PEOPLE ARE PLACED IN A ROW
Page 22

1 A is correct. Jan is furthest to the left.

If Ben is to the right of Jan, then Jan must be to the left of Ben. As he is also to the left of Mo, he must be furthest to the left. All other options are possible but not necessarily true.

2 D is correct. Bryan will speak first.

Graham, Heather and Calista were all drawn after other people so cannot be first. Therefore Bryan must have been drawn first and so will speak first. All other options are possible but not necessarily true.

SAMPLE TEST 1A Page 23

1 A **2** B **3** D **4** B **5** C **6** C **7** D **8** A **9** D
10 B **11** C **12** C **13** C **14** A **15** B

1 The only way the shape given can be used is if it is in one of the following arrangements. Two of the arrangements use the shapes from A.

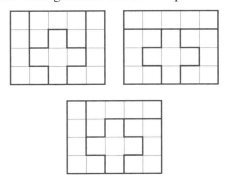

2 Troy uses correct reasoning when he predicts that Owen will get a book on Saturday if his mother earns a bonus. The information in the box says this is what happens.

A is incorrect. Natalie uses incorrect reasoning to claim that because Owen has a new book at school on Monday his mother **must** have earned a bonus. Owen might get new books at other times, for other reasons and from other people.

C and D are incorrect by a process of elimination.

3 It cannot be true that Maggie went to school in the car on Friday if it was not raining. She only goes to school by car on Thursdays or on rainy days.

A is incorrect. It could be true that it rained on Thursday so Maggie went to school by car.

B and C are incorrect. These could be true because Maggie goes to school by car when it is raining,

4 A sketch of the area could look like this. Town B is north-west of Town D.

● Town A

● Town B   ● Town C

● Town D

5 Tu uses mango and blueberries; neither Dean nor Iris uses these fruits.

A is incorrect. Tu does not use orange or peach.

B is incorrect. Tu does not use peach.

D is incorrect. Tu does not use pear.

6 The circuit must be completed by two tiles. One must have a 3 on it and the other must have a 1 on it. The two tiles must also share a number that can connect together. 2 and 4 share the number 4, one has a 3 and the other a 1.

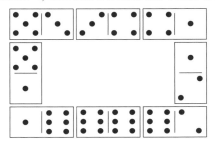

7 We know that both Oli and Jack are ahead of Will so he must be third in line.

Both A and B are possible but not necessarily true. C is not possible.

8 The creator of the text claims it's vital to save bogong moths from extinction. One reason given is that bogongs provide essential food for pygmy possums. The claim is strengthened by further information that suggests the pygmy possums will become extinct without bogong moths to eat.

B and D are incorrect. These statements are in the text.

C is incorrect. This statement might be true but it does not strengthen the specific claim about bogong months.

9 Aisha's conclusion is that Leon must get off the road. She based this conclusion on the evidence that there is a truck coming. So for her conclusion to work it must be assumed the truck is not going to stop. (There is a truck coming + the truck is not going to stop means therefore Leon must get off the road.)

A and C are incorrect. These assumptions do not support the conclusion that Leon must get off the road.

B is incorrect. This is Aisha's conclusion.

10 French, woodwork and sewing are all only available on lists 2 and 4. This means only two of these subjects can be chosen together. For example, if French is chosen from list 2 and woodwork is chosen from list 4, then sewing cannot be chosen at all. It is not possible to choose all three subjects.

11 The text is persuasive. It is trying to persuade people to get an ebike. This idea is supported by all the reasons given: they are fun; they keep you fit; they are a good method of transport; and they are kinder to the planet than petrol or diesel cars.

The other options are incorrect. These support the main idea as they are reasons to get an ebike but not the main idea of the text.

12 The main idea is that raptors are a special group of birds also known as birds of prey. C is the option that best expresses this. The rest of the text gives supporting information about raptors and their prey.

A and B are incorrect. This is supporting information for the main idea.

D is incorrect. This information is not in the text so it cannot be the main idea.

13 The period encompasses 14 days, as both Tuesday 3rd and Monday 16th are included. Over a period of 14 days, 14 shows are completed plus another 4 shows for the two Fridays and Saturdays.

14 According to the instructor, if a climber has not climbed all walls in the V0 to V2 range, they do not have a chance of passing the test to move onto V3 walls. Therefore none of the climbers who have not climbed all walls in the V0 to V2 range will pass the test. And since they won't pass the test, they won't be allowed to climb V3 walls.

B and D are incorrect. The instructor says climbers must have climbed those walls.

C is incorrect. According to the instructor, having climbed all those walls only gives a climber a **chance** of passing the test to then climb V3 walls. It does not guarantee a climber **can** move on to V3 walls.

15 After the first two steps, the square has sides that are half the side length of the original piece of paper. Once the steps are repeated the square will have side lengths one-quarter the length of the original piece. Multiplying the current side length by 4 will give the original side length: $5 \times 4 = 20$.

The following diagram shows the steps of the folding.

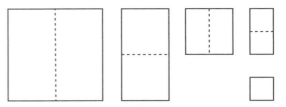

Each small square is 5 cm by 5 cm. The piece of paper is 20 cm by 20 cm.

SAMPLE TEST 1B Page 26

1 B 2 D 3 C 4 A 5 C 6 A 7 B 8 D 9 C
10 C 11 D 12 A 13 B 14 B 15 D

1 Thelma takes the wheel at 11.20 am.

The drive takes 10 hours in total, as there are 10 hours between 8 am and 6 pm. If Thelma is to drive for twice as long as Louise, then we split the drive into three sections. One will be completed by Louise and two will be completed by Thelma. We need to divide 10 hours into three parts.

$$10 \text{ hours} \div 3 = 3\frac{1}{3} \text{ hours}$$
$$= 3 \text{ hours } 20 \text{ minutes}$$

Louise will drive for 3 hours 20 minutes from 8 am. Thelma will take the wheel at 11.20 am and will drive for 6 hours 40 minutes until they stop at 6 pm.

2 Gabriel can't be certain that Lavinia tidied her room and washed the dog. Lavinia has to make her parents happy with her behaviour to be allowed to go to the party. Gabriel's reasoning is incorrect. There may be other ways to make her parents happy.

Tao cannot reason that just because Lavinia is not allowed to go to the party it's because she can't have tidied her room or washed the dog. There may be other reasons for Lavinia's parents to be unhappy with her behaviour. Tao's reasoning is incorrect.

3 A sketch of the area could look like this. Town D is north-west of Town C.

● Town A   ● Town E

● Town D   ● Town B   ● Town F

● Town C

4 Just because the backpack has a ribbon tied to its strap does not mean it has to be Melody's. Melody's might not be the only backpack with a red ribbon tied to the strap.

B is incorrect. This statement that Melody might be trying to steal someone else's backpack is not logical given the information in the text.

C is incorrect. The ribbon is the right colour (red) so this is not the mistake Rina has made.

D is incorrect. The statement that Melody might not be in the library when Rina and Stan get there might be true but it is not the mistake Rina has made.

5 Ariana is swimming fourth. Zianna swims ahead of Peyton, who swims ahead of Ariana. So Ariana swims third or fourth. But we also know that Caitlyn swims ahead of Ariana. So all three other girls swim before Ariana and so she must swim fourth. All options are possible but only C **must** be true.

6 The note will be 2 octaves higher.

Work out how many times 32 is halved to get to 8.

$$32 \div 2 = 16$$
$$16 \div 2 = 8$$

The string is halved in length twice, which means the note will be 2 octaves higher.

7 Millicent uses correct reasoning when she says the AB(E) extinguisher can be used if your curtains catch fire because this extinguisher can be used on fabric. Jacob uses correct reasoning when he says that if you have a wood fire and the fire gets out of control, you can use the AB(E) extinguisher because it is used on wood.

The other options are incorrect. Mira's reasoning is incorrect when she says you can use the AB(E) extinguisher in the kitchen if you have been frying chips and they catch fire. The sign says that the AB(E) extinguisher is not to be used on cooking oils. Harry uses incorrect reasoning when he says that if your electric blanket catches fire, you can use the foam extinguisher. The sign says that foam cannot be used on an electrical fire.

8 Flo cannot be seated next to Cam. Once Ann and Don are placed, Bea can be placed in any of the remaining seats. El must be on the other side of the table, as she cannot be placed next to Bea. Two of the remaining seats are filled by Cam and Flo but they are never next to each other. Cam can be seated next to all other people as shown in the two possible arrangements below.

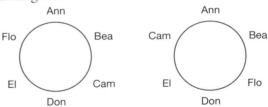

9 The argument is that carrots are good for you so you should eat some every day. This argument is not true for people with an allergy to carrots so the statement that carrot allergies are rare but some people can have an allergic reaction to carrots weakens the argument.

A and D are incorrect. These statements strengthen any argument to eat carrots.

B is incorrect. This statement is already in the text and so does not weaken the argument.

10 Domino 3 cannot be used as it contains a 6, which cannot be used in either position in the bottom space, and a 3, which cannot be used in either position in the top space. The other combinations all work.

11 Miley uses parsley and roast pumpkin; neither Claudia nor Greg use those ingredients in their salads.

A is incorrect. Claudia also uses olives.

B is incorrect. Miley does not use radishes and Greg also uses red onion.

C is incorrect. Claudia uses olives and Miley does not use grated carrot.

12 Jimmy will make 10 visits. The holiday period includes two full weeks from Saturday 9th to Friday 22nd, plus the last two days of the holiday, Saturday 23rd and Sunday 24th. So Jimmy makes the four visits per week for the first two weeks plus a visit on the Saturday and Sunday at the end of the holidays. $4 + 4 + 2 = 10$

13 Salad and cheese and crackers are both included in the lunchbox on Monday. But neither the Wednesday lunchbox nor the Friday lunchbox includes either one.

A is incorrect. A cookie and salad are both included in the lunchbox on Monday, and neither Wednesday's lunchbox nor Friday's lunchbox has a salad. However, Friday's lunchbox includes a cookie.

C is incorrect. Djurdja's mother did not take trail mix and a sandwich on Monday.

D is incorrect. Cheese and crackers and an apple are both included in the lunchbox on Monday but both Wednesday's and Friday's lunchbox also includes an apple.

14 The arrangements for the other options are shown here. There is no solution for B.

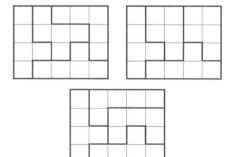

15 The main idea is that the fire station has been upgraded. Option D is the one that best expresses this. The rest of the text gives supporting information about why the station was upgraded and the features of the upgrade.

A **is incorrect.** This is supporting information for the main idea, explaining why the station was upgraded.

B is incorrect. This information is not in the text so cannot be the main idea.

C is incorrect. This is supporting information for the main idea, detailing one of the features of the upgrade.

SAMPLE TEST 2A
Page 29

1 A **2** C **3** B **4** C **5** C **6** D **7** C **8** B **9** D
10 C **11** A **12** B **13** B **14** C **15** A

1 To answer this question it is best to list all possible orders of the cards. Because the King is immediately to the left of the Queen we can treat those two cards as a single unit. By placing the Ace and Jack around them with the Jack always to the right of the Ace, the three possible orders are:

KQ – A – J

A – KQ – J

A – J – KQ

King, Queen, Ace, Jack

Ace, King, Queen, Jack

Ace, Jack, King, Queen

The Ace is never in the second position from the left.

2 The creator of the text claims the Mona Lisa is one of the most famous and valuable artworks in the world. The statement that confirms the fame and value of the work is the fact that it is kept behind bulletproof glass.

A is incorrect. This statement is in the text so it does not strengthen the claim.

B and D are incorrect. These statements might be true but do not strengthen the claim about the Mona Lisa being famous and valuable.

3 Eli cannot claim that **all** bestselling books make successful films because not every bestselling book is made into a movie.

The other options are incorrect. These statements might be true but are not the mistake Eli has made.

4 The diagram of his walk is shown below. He is 100 m north of his starting point so must walk 100 m south to get there. Each large gridline is 100 m from the next one.

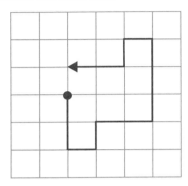

5 If you need an opportunity and a motive to have untied the goat then anyone without an opportunity cannot have been the one to untie the goat.

A and B are incorrect. These statements are not logical.

D is incorrect. If Joo had an opportunity and a motive, he could have been the one to untie the goat.

6 Percussion must be chosen from list 3 as it is only available there. This means that clarinet must be chosen from list 4 as it cannot be chosen from list 3. Trumpet can be chosen from either list 1 or list 2, which means any instrument from those lists are available. The oboe only appears in lists 3 and 4 so it is impossible for Birgitte to choose it.

7 Maia completed the race in 5 hours, as there are 5 hours between 9 am and 2 pm. If Alex completed the race four times faster, then we need to find one-quarter of 5 hours.

$$5 \text{ hours} \div 4 = 1.25 \text{ hours}$$
$$= 1 \text{ hour } 15 \text{ minutes}$$

So Alex completed the race in 1 hour 15 minutes and crossed the finish line at 10.15 am.

8 The information tells you the flavour of a blood orange is similar to that of a ruby grapefruit or an orange with a hint of raspberry. To substitute a blood orange in a recipe you need to use an orange and some raspberries to balance the sweetness with the

flavour and to add colour. Annchi used incorrect reasoning to declare that substituting a blood orange with a white grapefruit for flavour and strawberries for colour **will** work.

A is incorrect. Hugo uses correct reasoning when he recognises his mistake that substituting a white grapefruit for a blood orange is what made his juice too sour.

C and D are incorrect by a process of elimination.

9 If Shawn is not invited, then you know Camilla will be invited. And if Camilla is invited, then Zi will invite Yan and not Benny. The answer is Camilla and Yan.

The other options are incorrect by a process of elimination.

10 Here is the solution for C.

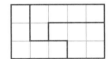

There are no solutions for the other shapes.

11 The radio station claims everyone in the area should prepare for bushfire season by making a survival plan. The rest of the announcement supports this claim by stating some of the benefits of having a plan. The statement that having a plan can save lives further supports the claim.

B is incorrect. This statement could support the claim that everyone should make a plan, since it is so quick and easy to do so. However, it is not the statement that best supports the claim.

C and D are incorrect. These statements do not support the claim that everyone should make a survival plan.

12 We know that Conner's mum always rearranges the furniture when she's in a bad mood and she's always in a bad mood when she doesn't finish a marathon. So Conner's reasoning is correct.

A is incorrect. Saane has not thought there might be other reasons why Conner's mum is in a bad mood causing her to rearrange the furniture. Also there might be other reasons why she rearranged the furniture, other than because she is in a bad mood.

C and D are incorrect by a process of elimination.

13 The building has five rooms. This rules out A as it only has four rooms. The two largest rooms occupy opposite corners of the building. This rules out C and D. B is the answer.

14 For Felicity's conclusion that we must remove the plastic rubbish to hold, it must be assumed that removing the plastic would be a good thing. (The oceans are filled with plastic rubbish + removing plastic from the oceans would be a good thing means therefore we must remove the plastic rubbish.)

A is incorrect. This is the conclusion Felicity drew, based on the evidence that the oceans are filled with plastic and the assumption that removing the plastic would be a good thing.

B is incorrect. This is the evidence Felicity used to support her conclusion.

D is incorrect. This assumption does not support Felicity's conclusion that we must remove the plastic.

15 Once Lila and Matt are placed, the seat directly between them must be occupied by either Quin or Nala because otherwise these two cannot be directly opposite each other. The two remaining seats, which are not next to each other, must be occupied by Peta and Orla. So Orla cannot be sitting next to Peta. Peta can be seated next to every other person, as shown in the following diagrams.

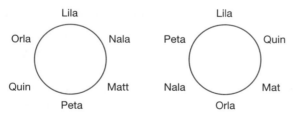

SAMPLE TEST 2B
Page 32

1 B 2 C 3 C 4 B 5 A 6 A 7 D 8 B 9 A
10 D 11 D 12 C 13 C 14 B 15 A

1 Quoits must be played at 11 am, as it is not available any other time. That means hopscotch must be played at midday.

2 It cannot be true that Mr Xu would call practices on Tuesday and Wednesday for the whole orchestra. That would mean the strings section of the orchestra would practise two days in a row and the information tells you this never happens.

The other options are incorrect. These statements could be true.

3 It took Bree 1 hour (60 minutes) to walk into town. If Fleur is five times closer and walks at the same speed, it will take her one-fifth of the time.

$$60 \text{ minutes} \div 5 = 12 \text{ minutes}$$

It took her 12 minutes to walk and she arrived at 2 pm. 12 minutes before 2 pm is 1.48 pm.

4 Mum says Tori will need to do homework for **at least** one hour every night from Monday to Thursday but only doing one hour does not mean Tori can say she will definitely get all her homework done.

A and D are incorrect. These statements might be true but are not the mistake Tori has made.

C is incorrect. This statement is what Tori thinks is true so does not show her mistake.

5 If Poppy is 3 rooms from Bec, they are in room 1 and room 4 or room 2 and room 5. If Jen is next to Til they must occupy the two rooms between Poppy and Bec. Kim must be in the remaining room and Jen must be two rooms away in room 3.

	Room 1	Room 2	Room 3	Room 4	Room 5
Option A	Poppy	Til	Jen	Bec	Kim
Option B	Bec	Til	Jen	Poppy	Kim
Option C	Kim	Bec	Jen	Til	Poppy
Option D	Kim	Poppy	Jen	Til	Bec

Of the four, Til cannot be in room 1.

6 The building has five rooms. This rules out B and D as they have six rooms each. The compound shape that is made up of three rectangles stretches from one side of the building to the other and also extends out to a third side. This rules out C.

7 The creator of the text wants you to accept that you should use more herbs and spices in your cooking for all the health benefits and the added flavour.

A and B are incorrect. These statements provide additional information not stated in the text so they cannot be the main idea of the text.

C is incorrect. It supports the main idea of the text.

8 William played on 13 days.

In a normal week, William plays sports on five days: Monday, Tuesday, Wednesday, Thursday and Saturday. From Monday 11 to Sunday 24 there are two weeks, each with five days of sport. We need to add on Wednesday 6, Thursday 7 and Saturday 9 before this to get the total.

$$3 + 2 \times 5 = 3 + 10$$
$$= 13$$

9 Jhulan's argument is that healthy soil is vital to support life on Earth. The statement that best supports the claim is that healthy soil is vital to grow food.

B is incorrect. It is a fact in the text so does not add anything new to support the argument.

C and D are incorrect. These statements support the argument but not as strongly as A.

10 The solutions for the other options are shown below.

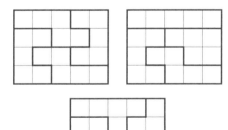

There is no solution for D.

11 Both Adriana and Lulu use incorrect reasoning. Adriana cannot be **sure** that all the city's coffee shops would need to have been involved in the competition. Lulu cannot reasonably say **for sure** that only Ray's family members and friends would have been allowed to vote.

The other options are incorrect. Casey demonstrates an understanding that the vote might have been limited so that the outcome was one that Rays wanted and could use in advertising so Casey's reasoning is correct. Tevita expresses a personal opinion based on experience so her reasoning is correct.

12 The circuit must be completed by two dominoes. The dominoes must share a number that can connect together. The other numbers must be a 5 and a 3 so the dominoes can connect to the remainder of the circuit. All options except for C follow this rule.

13 Emmeline's mother claims that Australians need to reduce the amount of food they waste. She supports this claim by saying how many kilos of food are thrown out by an average household in a year. The statement that a study found an average of $965 per person per year is spent on wasted food further supports the claim.

A is incorrect. This statement gives further information about what is thrown out—but not the amount. So it does not **best** support the claim.

B and D are incorrect. These statements give an example of something people could do to reduce waste but do not support the claim that people **need** to reduce that waste.

14 Once the first fold is made we have two triangles. Every time we fold in half from now on we double the number of triangles. We are told the paper is folded four more times so we must double 2 four times.

2 triangles $\times 2 \times 2 \times 2 \times 2 = 32$ triangles

Try it yourself with a large piece of square paper.

15 Only Lucas's reasoning is correct. We know that only students who attended every club meeting last term will be allowed to enter the challenge this term. So, since Lucas missed a meeting last term, he will not be allowed to enter.

B is incorrect. Even though Olivia attended every meeting last term, there may be other reasons why some students are unable to enter the challenge. So, it is a flaw in her reasoning to say she will **definitely** be entering.

C and D are incorrect by a process of elimination.

SAMPLE TEST 3A

Page 36

1 C **2** A **3** D **4** C **5** D **6** B **7** D **8** B **9** D **10** D **11** C **12** C **13** A **14** A **15** C

1 Remember that a shorter time is better in races. Tori improved by 19.3−16.5 = 2.8 seconds. Using the same process we can see that Leila improved by 2.5 seconds, Ashlyn by 1.8, Akaya by 1.0 and Keisha by 1.5 seconds. Tori was the most improved.

2 The creator of the text claims that shark finning is cruel, wasteful and bad for the marine ecosystem. Any further evidence that includes why or how shark finning is bad will strengthen the argument. Sharks are essential for a healthy marine environment so killing them is bad for the marine ecosystem.

B is incorrect. This statement is already a fact in the text.

C is incorrect. This statement might be true but does not add to the claim about shark finning.

D is incorrect. This statement is irrelevant to the claim.

3 Tao's reasoning is incorrect. The instructions in the box say to allow the butter to soften out of the fridge then it will beat smoothly with the sugar. If the butter is lumpy, it must be because the butter was too hard rather than too soft as Tao suggested.

The other options are incorrect because the reasoning is correct.

4 The argument is in favour of reducing a speed limit to 40 km per hour from 60 km per hour. The evidence to support the argument is that three recent accidents involved vehicles travelling in excess of 90 km per hour. Reducing the speed from 60 to 40 km per hour would not have prevented the three accidents Serena mentions as those vehicles were travelling considerably faster than the speed limit of 60 km per hour.

5 The domino that goes in the space on the side cannot have a 4 as it will be touching another 4. Dominoes 1 and 3 both have a 4 on them so they cannot be used as one of them will have to be used in the space on the side. All other options are possible.

6 All four have the same top view. D does not have the correct front view so can be ruled out. C does not have the correct right view so can be ruled out. A has the reflection of the correct right view but that would mean viewing it from the back which we are not doing. It can also be ruled out. This leaves B.

7 Jamal can never sit in the second space from the left.

If Jamal sits in the second space from the left then one of the other friends must sit in the first space on the left. But this is impossible as they must be sitting next to one of the other students. For example, if Penny is sitting in the first space on the left, Farrah must be seated in the second space. So Jamal cannot be sitting there.

8 Josh has concluded that a dog named Bonsai must be small because a bonsai is a small tree. To draw this conclusion he must have assumed only small dogs are named after small things. (The evidence that the dog's name is Bonsai plus Josh's assumption that only small dogs are named after small things leads Josh to conclude that Bonsai must be a small dog. Note that Josh's conclusion might be based on an incorrect assumption.)

A and C are incorrect. These statements are not assumptions Josh has made.

D is incorrect. This statement is irrelevant to the question.

9 If the person who moved Doug's canoe along the beach needed to have an opportunity and a motive, anyone without a motive cannot have been the person to move it.

A is incorrect. Anita might have had a motive but still not moved the canoe.

B is incorrect. Anita might have had an opportunity but still not moved the canoe.

C is incorrect. Anita might have had an opportunity and a motive but this doesn't mean she must have been the one to move the canoe.

10 A sketch of the area could look like this. Town F is south-east of Town A.

● Town B

● Town D   ● Town A

● Town C   ● Town F

● Town E

11 The sales assistant has found a toy that matches the description from Ash's niece and assumes it **must** be the one she wants. However, it might not be the correct toy because there could be other dinosaurs with yellow spots.

A is incorrect. Even if this is true, it is not a mistake made by the sales assistant.

B is incorrect. The sales assistant says the toy has yellow spots.

D is incorrect. Ash is in the toy store mentioned by her niece.

12 Inground jumping pad and climbing net are both included in the list of things Hugo wants in a playground but neither Santi nor Alex mentions either one.

A is incorrect. Hugo wants a curved slide and inground jumping pad but Alex would also like a curved slide.

B is incorrect. Hugo wants a climbing net and swings but both Santi and Alex would also like a climbing net and swings.

D is incorrect. Hugo doesn't say he wants a nature trail and timber boat.

13 Glenda cannot choose oil painting.

Watercolour is only available from list 3. This means sculpture must be chosen from list 1 and ceramics must be from list 4. Glenda must make her last selection from list 2. Oil painting is not on this list so she cannot possibly choose it.

14 David's conclusion is that they should sit near the door of the bus. He has based this conclusion on the evidence that it's faster to get off the bus if you sit near the door. So, for his conclusion to work, it must be assumed that getting off the bus quickly will be a good thing.

(It's faster to get off the bus if you sit near the door + getting off the bus quickly will be a good thing means therefore they should sit near the door.)

B is incorrect. This is David's conclusion.

C is incorrect. This assumption does not support David's conclusion. (It's faster to get off the bus if you sit near the door + the bus is empty does not mean therefore they should sit near the door.)

D is incorrect. This is the evidence David used.

15 March has 31 days and April has 30 days. Together this is 61 days. How many weeks (7 days) go into 61 days? There are 8 full weeks and 5 days left over. As the first of those weeks starts on a Monday, so do the final 5 days. They are Monday to Friday and include four days in which Kelly is teaching. Kelly teaches 4 days a week and an extra Sunday every month. We need to add the total of 8 full weeks to the 4 days from the final 5 days and the 2 extra Sunday lessons.

$$8 \times 4 + 4 + 2 = 38$$

SAMPLE TEST 3B   Page 40

> **1** D **2** A **3** D **4** D **5** B **6** A **7** B **8** B **9** C
> **10** A **11** B **12** C **13** B **14** C **15** D

1 The journey takes 5.5 hours (5 hours 30 minutes) one way. Together the two journeys take 11 hours. $5.5 + 5.5 = 11$ and the hour wait at Marseille makes the total time 12 hours between leaving and arriving in Paris. The train arrives at 7 pm.

2 You are told that '[b]y 1937 the speed limit in built-up areas had been gradually increased to 50 kilometres per hour, while 80 kilometres per hour was the limit on open roads'. The only conclusion possible is that cars were allowed to travel faster in non–built up areas.

The other options are incorrect. It is not possible to draw these conclusions from the evidence in the text. You could only state that they are likely to be true.

3 The sphere is not as wide as the widest stretch across the hexagonal prism. In D the sphere is as wide. The other three options are all views of the solid.

4 Neither Tariq nor Willem grow spring onions or cos lettuce.

The other options are incorrect by a process of elimination.

5 A green must be next to a blue.

All options are possible. However, if the greens are not next to each other, as the question states, there are at least three beads that are next to a green. At least one of these must be blue, as there are only two yellow beads.

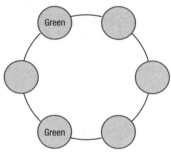

6 If the square is on the top, the circle must be on the right and the octagon on the left. This is the reverse of what is shown on A.

7 If Dad eats chocolate, he's **sure** to have too little sleep so will not be able to do his job effectively and therefore he'll get grumpy and won't allow the children to stay up late to watch their favourite shows the next night. Beth's reasoning is correct.

A is incorrect. You are told the children miss out on staying up to watch their favourite shows when Dad gets grumpy from eating chocolate but there could have been other reasons why the children were not allowed to stay up to watch TV on Tuesday night. Therefore Taane's reasoning is incorrect.

C and D are incorrect by a process of elimination.

8 Bella is sitting in the left window seat.

As Chris is sitting on Bella's left, only he or Anna can be sitting in the left window seat. Bella cannot be seated there. All other options are possible.

9 The creator of the text claims that more must be done to protect wildlife from cats. Supporting evidence tells of the numbers of wild animals killed by cats so option C strengthens the claim.

It provides further evidence that cats are a threat to wildlife, not just because they hunt and kill but because they compete for food and shelter.

The other options might be true but these statements do not **most** strengthen the claim.

10 Some solutions for the other options are shown below.

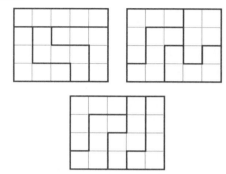

There is no solution for A.

11 Since everyone had to vote for two of the topics, knowing that no student voted for both exercise and TV tells you every student must have voted for the homework topic.

A is incorrect. Knowing this does not allow you to know the result of the vote.

C is incorrect. This only tells you exercise was one of the top two answers.

D is incorrect. This information only tells you TV could not have won the vote. It does not allow you to know the result of the vote. The topic for the debate will be 'Does homework support learning?'

12 Starting on Tuesday 7, and for three weeks afterwards until Tuesday 28, each week includes four shifts except for the week that includes Wednesday 15. The last few days are Tuesday 28, Wednesday 29 and Thursday 30. Altogether Helmut has worked 14 shifts.

$$3 \times 4 + 3 - 1 = 14$$

13 If Melia does not sing, you can conclude that Alice will sing and if Alice sings, Ben will sing in place of Joe.

A is incorrect. If Alice sings, Ben will sing in place of Joe.

C is incorrect. If Melia does not sing, you can conclude that Alice will sing and if Alice sings, Joe will be replaced with Ben.

D is incorrect. Since Alice will sing, you can conclude that Ben will sing but Joe won't.

14 The diagram of their walks is shown below. Each large gridline is 100 m from the next one.

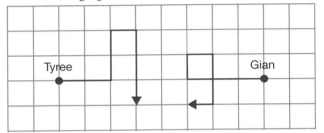

15 The main idea is that a robot nicknamed 'BeachBot' has been designed to clean up beach litter. Option D is the statement that best expresses this. The rest of the text gives supporting information about BeachBot.

A and C are incorrect. This is supporting information for the main idea.

B is incorrect. This information is not in the text so cannot be the main idea.

SAMPLE TEST 4A

Page 44

1 B 2 A 3 A 4 B 5 D 6 D 7 C 8 C 9 C
10 B 11 A 12 B 13 B 14 D 15 D

1 Pain-Away is the least expensive brand. The other options are all possible but not necessarily true.

2 Nils has concluded that a dog called Brutus must be big and scary. The evidence for Nils's conclusion is that Brutus is the name of the dog and, to Nils, Brutus sounds like brute. Nils's assumption must be that any dog with a big, scary-sounding name must be big and scary.

C is incorrect. This might be true but this is not the assumption Nils has made.

B and D are incorrect. These statements are irrelevant to the assumption.

3 It takes the fast train 5 hours to make the trip. It takes the slow train three times as long. 3 × 5 = 15 hours. 15 hours after 5 pm is 8 am the next day.

4 You are told that only dogs which have earned an Obedience Certificate from the dog training school will be **allowed to try out** next week for

work as security dogs. Cody is correct that Yumi's dog will not be able to get security work because it can't try out without a certificate.

A is incorrect. Ellyse is incorrect in asserting that Max's dog will be given security work. It may have earned an Obedience Certificate but might not get security work in spite of the certificate. It will only be trying out next week. There is no guarantee it will be successful.

C and D are incorrect by a process of elimination.

5 The creator of the text wants you to accept the argument that volcano tourism is popular but not without risk. To weaken this argument you would need evidence of reduced risk. The statement that volcanologists can usually predict if a volcano is about to erupt means people can be warned and evacuated in time to save lives.

The other options add information about volcanoes but do not weaken the argument.

6 Toni is 200 m east of Francis

The diagram of their walks is shown below. Each large gridline is 100m from the next one.

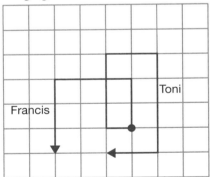

7 Zilla is sitting between Brienne and Cristo.

The second sentence tells us that Eloise and Zilla must be on the long sides of the table as they cannot be 'diagonally' opposite anyone if they are on the ends.

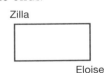

The third sentence tells us Mika and Cristo must be on the ends as they are directly opposite each other. As Mika is next to Eloise and Rachel is next to Cristo, the diagram below shows where they must sit in relation to each other.

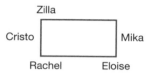

Brienne must therefore sit next to Zilla, as shown. Zilla sits between Brienne and Cristo.

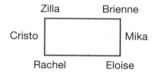

Zilla and Eloise could have been placed on different ends or sides of the table to begin with but Zilla will still be between Brienne and Cristo.

8 Piper's conclusion is incorrect. The information in the box tells you the antechinus is an Australian native mouse that is sometimes mistaken for a common non-native mouse.

The other options are incorrect. These statements are correct: Ye and Viraj give their opinions and Anthony makes a statement of fact.

9 The text tells that working as a wildlife carer can be stressful but also rewarding. Evidence that it can be stressful includes the statement that carers were worried the koala burned in the bushfire would not survive. Evidence that it is rewarding is that the injured koala was released back into the wild and has had a baby.

The other options are incorrect. They provide supporting information rather than express the main idea.

10 English, woodwork and engineering must be chosen in some way from lists 1, 2 and 4 as they don't appear in list 3. This means the only options for Kara's fourth subject must come from list 3. As computers does not appear in list 3 it is impossible for her to choose it.

11 Uma's main idea is that she loves cats and A is the option that best expresses this. This idea is mentioned in the first sentence and reinforced in the final sentence. The rest of the text gives more information about why Uma loves cats and who doesn't love cats.

B is incorrect. This is supporting information for the main idea.

C and D are incorrect. This information is not in the text so cannot be the main idea.

12 Lucia's conclusion is that Sajid's father has a good imagination. She has based this conclusion on the evidence that he is an author. So, for her conclusion to hold, it must be assumed that all authors have good imaginations. (Sajid's father is an author + all authors have good imaginations means therefore Sajid's father has a good imagination.)

A is incorrect. This assumption would not support Lucia's conclusion that Sajid's father must have a good imagination.

B is incorrect. This is Lucia's conclusion, not her assumption.

D is incorrect. This is the evidence Lucia has used to base her conclusion on.

13 Kai missed 17 sessions.

Kai trains 9 times a week: 3 days with 2 sessions and 3 days with 1 session. If he was away for the full two weeks from Wednesday 7 to the end of Tuesday 20, he would have missed two weeks of training. Instead he returned one day earlier and was able to get to his training session on Tuesday 20.

$$2 \times 9 - 1 = 17$$

We can multiply 9 by the two weeks and then take away the Tuesday session that he gets back in time for.

14 According to the teacher if a student has not been at practice at least once a week for eight weeks, they do not have a chance of passing the exam. Therefore none of the students who come to practice less than once a week for eight weeks will pass the exam.

A is incorrect. According to the teacher, coming to practice at least once a week for eight weeks gives a student only a **chance** of passing the exam. It does not guarantee a pass.

B is incorrect. This is the minimum required to have a **chance** of passing. It does not guarantee a pass.

C is incorrect. The teacher says students **must** have been to practice at least once a week for eight weeks so if a student has come to less practices than this, they cannot pass.

D is incorrect. This does not support Anya's claim about therapy dogs being a good idea.

15 Compare each shape in the question diagram with each option and work out which option has all five shapes.

SAMPLE TEST 4B
Page 47

1 D 2 C 3 B 4 D 5 A 6 C 7 C 8 D 9 C
10 A 11 D 12 B 13 D 14 A 15 A

1 The solutions for the other shapes are below.

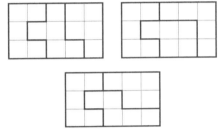

There is no solution for D.

2 Both Frankie and Rose use correct reasoning. They use information in the text to correctly identify traits of seals and sea lions and each only states what they **think** each animal is. Neither asserts that they definitely **know** what the animals are.

3 Lauren missed 11 gym sessions.

Lauren usually attends the gym 6 times per week: every weekday and twice on Thursday. If she was away from Monday 9, she would miss two weeks of training sessions. Instead she is able to make the training session on that Monday. So the number of sessions she misses is given by:

$$2 \times 6 - 1 = 12 - 1$$
$$= 11 \text{ sessions.}$$

4 Neither Timothy nor Mira has stamps from Northern Ireland or Wales.

5 Dimitri will be unable to see Iron Man.

Batman is on in session 1 and 4. As Dimitri wants to see the Batman films in order he must watch Batman in session 1. This means he must watch Spiderman in session 4 and Batman 2 in session 3. His fourth film must be picked from

session 2. Iron Man is not on that list so it is not possible for Dimitri to see it.

6 If the second ball showed a higher number than 5 then statement C is true. If the second ball showed a lower number than 5 and then it struck the 8-ball, statement C would again be true. Statement C must be true. All other options are possible, but we cannot say that they **must** be true.

7 Zane has concluded he will buy black nail polish for his mum for her birthday. He has drawn this conclusion based on the evidence that Mum loves black clothes and that she wears nail polish. Zane's assumption must be that she will like black nail polish.

A and B are incorrect. These statements are in the text so are not assumptions.

D is incorrect. This could be true but it is not an assumption Zane has made.

8 The white envelope is two spaces from the grey which is in the middle of the row, so the white one must be at the end of the row. The blue and pink envelopes must be in positions 2 and 4 as otherwise they cannot be two spaces from one another. As the red must be next to the blue, the red must be at the end of the row next to the blue. The two options for the arrangement are below. In both, the code is in the pink envelope.

White	Pink	Grey	Blue	Red

Red	Blue	Grey	Pink	White

9 The creator of the text wants you to accept the argument that butterflies are essential in the food chain and for pollinating plants. The statement that best supports the argument is that nearly two thirds of invertebrates need butterflies in the food chain in order to survive.

A and B are incorrect. These statements do not strengthen the argument. They are ways to help butterflies.

D is incorrect. This statement does not strengthen the argument. It is a fact about butterflies.

10 B, C and D are all views of the solid. B is the view from the front right, C is the view from the front left and D is the view from the top. A is not a view of the solid.

11 Mr Thomas believes that because only twenty students were wearing their coloured clothes, the other seven students in his class must have brought coloured clothes to change into. His mistake is that some of the students might have forgotten it was a team games day and forgotten to wear or bring coloured clothes at all.

The other options are incorrect. They are irrelevant to the mistake Mr Thomas has made.

12 Town D must be due east of Town C. It is north-east of Town C in the diagram. Every other diagram is possible.

13 Neither Ella nor Anh is correct.

A is incorrect. Even though Ella has already handed in her permission note, there may be other reasons why some students are not allowed to go on the excursion. Therefore it is a flaw in her reasoning to say she will **definitely** be able to go.

B is incorrect. Anh forgot his note today but he has until tomorrow to hand it in. So he may still be allowed to go on the excursion.

C is incorrect by a process of elimination.

14 If Usain is inside Asafa then Asafa is outside Usain. Asafa is also outside Donovan so Asafa must be in the outside lane. Therefore he cannot be between the other two runners. Asafa is between Usain and Donovan.

15 Katy's conclusion is that Harry really likes bananas. She has based this conclusion on the evidence that Harry has had a banana for lunch two days running. So, for her conclusion to hold, it must be assumed that anyone who has a banana for lunch two days running must really like bananas. (Harry has had a banana for lunch two days running + anyone who has a banana for lunch two days running must really like bananas means therefore Harry really likes bananas.)

B is incorrect. This is Katy's conclusion.

C is incorrect. This is the evidence Katy has used to draw her conclusion.

D is incorrect. This would not support Katy's conclusion.

SAMPLE TEST 5A

Page 51

1 D **2** D **3** B **4** B **5** A **6** A **7** A **8** C **9** D
10 D **11** D **12** B **13** C **14** C **15** D

1 Here is the solution for D.

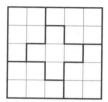

There are no solutions for the other shapes.

2 Arya uses flawed reasoning. All drummers are percussionists but not all percussionists play the drums.

The other options are incorrect. These statements could all be true so the reasoning is correct and not flawed.

3 Since everyone had to vote for two options out of the three, knowing that no-one voted for both fan and air conditioning, and air conditioning only, tells you that everyone voted for air conditioning. Air conditioning only must be the one everyone voted for because every option got at least one vote.

4 To answer this question it is best to list all possible orders for the friends. As Terry is immediately to the right of Jim, we can treat those two as a single unit. By placing Grant and Malcolm around them with Grant always further to the left than Malcolm, the three possible orders are:

G – M – JT

G – JT – M

JT – G – M

So the order could be:

Grant	Malcolm	Jim	Terry
Grant	Jim	Terry	Malcolm
Jim	Terry	Grant	Malcolm.

Malcolm can never be in the third position from the left.

5 The dietician wants people to accept the argument that children need to learn how to eat healthily and to cook healthy food in school. The statement that most strengthens the argument is that learning how to cook improves children's understanding of healthy eating.

The other options are incorrect. These statements might be true but they are not supportive of the argument.

6 If the circle is on the top and the pentagon is on the right side, the shape on the left side should be the hexagon, not the square. A is not a possible view of the dice.

7 D is the view from the back right. B is the view from the front right. C is the view from the bottom. A is not a view of the solid.

8 Erica has concluded that Blake must hate doing homework. Her evidence is that Blake never does his homework. Her assumption must be that people don't do things they hate doing. Note that Erica has made an assumption that may or may not be correct.

The other options are incorrect. These statements might be true but are not assumptions Erica has made.

9 The main idea is that fossil remains of a dinosaur suggest the type of food the dinosaur ate. The rest of the text details the kinds of teeth needed to eat the different kinds of food.

A and C are incorrect. They are facts in the text but not the main idea.

B is incorrect. It provides extra information about scientists so is not the main idea in the text.

10 Morse code and map reading are both only available in session 1 and session 3. This means they must be done in those sessions. Finding water is also only available in session 1 and session 3. So Fatma is unable to choose it. The other courses are all possible as fire building can be taken in session 2 or session 4.

11 Terry's conclusion is that they had better not break any windows. He has based this conclusion on the evidence that Mr Small will be angry if they break a window. So, for his conclusion to hold, it must be assumed it is they who must not do anything to make Mr Small angry. (Mr Small will be angry if they break a window + they must not do anything to make Mr Small angry means therefore they had better not break any windows.)

A is incorrect. This is Terry's conclusion, not his assumption.

B is incorrect. This assumption does not support Terry's conclusion that they had better not break any windows.

C is incorrect. This is the evidence Terry has used to base his conclusion on.

12 Gemma's father claims that a scarf is easier to knit than a blanket. The statement that he has chosen a complicated pattern most weakens this claim.

A and D are incorrect. These statements neither weaken nor support the claim that a scarf is easier to knit than a blanket.

C is incorrect. This statement could support the claim, rather than weaken it.

13 Chantelle will ride 17 times.

Chantelle rides twice per week. September has 30 days and October has 31 days. Together this is 61 days. How many weeks (7 days) go into 61 days? $8 \times 7 = 56$ so there are 8 full weeks and 5 days left over. The 5 days must start on a Thursday with the fifth day being a Monday which must be 31 October. In these five days Chantelle only rides on the Saturday.

The total number of rides she does is given by:

$$8 \text{ weeks} \times 2 \text{ rides} + 1 \text{ ride} = 16 \text{ rides} + 1 \text{ ride}$$
$$= 17 \text{ rides}$$

14 From Mira and Lee's descriptions we know the fruit on the tree is orange, round and very small. So, based on the information in the box, it could be a cumquat tree. However, it could also be a mandarin tree with young, smaller fruit. So Mira is correct when she says it **might** be a mandarin tree and Lee is also correct when he says it **could** be a cumquat tree.

The other options are incorrect by a process of elimination.

15 Kareem finds vanilla cake.

The rectangular box is 4 spaces from the square box. This means they are at either end of the row. The circular box which is 3 spaces from the rectangular box must therefore be next to the square box. The triangle is next to the circle, in the middle of the row, and the hexagon goes in the remaining spot.

Here are the two possible arrangements (one is a reflection of the other):

If the vanilla cake is three spaces from the chocolate, the chocolate cannot be in the middle of the row. So if it is next to the circle, which we are told it is, it must be in the square box. This means the vanilla is three spaces away inside the hexagonal box.

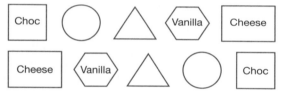

SAMPLE TEST 5B   Page 55

1 D 2 D 3 C 4 D 5 C 6 B 7 A 8 B 9 D
10 C 11 D 12 A 13 B 14 A 15 C

1 Mitch lives west of Ash. Bonnie lives east of Mitch so he lives west of Bonnie. If two people must be east of him, then he can never occupy the two easternmost houses in the street. He cannot live in the house furthest to the east or in the second house to the east.

2 Since whoever took Riku's lunch must have had an opportunity and a motive, then anyone who did not have an opportunity to take it cannot have been the one to have taken it. Therefore D cannot be true.

The other options are incorrect. These statements could each be true and so are incorrect answers.

3 Gordon cannot choose Thai. Moroccan must be chosen in session 3, which means German must be chosen in session 1. As Thai is only available in those sessions, it is not able to be chosen. The other three options can all be the fourth cuisine as Vietnamese can be chosen in session 2 or session 4.

4 Neither Carl nor Doris wants to visit the Philippines and Cambodia, whereas Ronald does.

5 To finish the race, Perry must run 80 metres 10 times, as $80 \times 10 = 800$.

When he crosses the line, Animesh will have run 75 metres 10 times: $75 \times 10 = 750$.

So Animesh will have run 750 metres and will have 50 metres to go.

6 28 days is exactly four weeks so will only ever have 12 sessions, as $4 \times 3 = 12$. To have one more training session, we need more days in the month. If the month starts on a Tuesday, we only need one more day, a Tuesday.

Su	M	Tu	W	Th	F	Sa
27	31	1	2	3	4	5
6	7	8	9	10	11	12
13	14	15	16	17	18	19
20	21	22	23	24	25	26
27	28	29	30	31	1	2

As you can see from the calendar above, if there were 28 days in the month, Jenna would have trained 12 times. With 29 days, she trains 13 times. Had the month had 30 or 31 days, she would have trained 14 or 15 days respectively.

7 The statement that the phone is in excellent condition best supports Bradley's ability to sell it.

B is incorrect. The statement that the phone is only three years old might make it unappealing to some buyers.

C and D are incorrect because this is irrelevant information.

8 The argument the creator of the text wants you to accept is that eels have an amazing migration story. The rest of the information tells all about this amazing migration.

A is incorrect. This is true but not the main idea of the text.

C is incorrect. This statement is expressed in the text but the text is about the migration pattern so this is not the main idea.

D is incorrect. This statement is expressed in the text but is not the main idea.

9 A is the view from the back left. C is the view from the top or bottom. B is the view from the back right. D is not a view of the solid.

10 Lenny uses incorrect reasoning. The fact that the bird is big and strong looking does not mean it **must** be an eagle. The information only states that 'eagles tend to be larger and more powerful than hawks'. Jennifer uses incorrect reasoning when she says the bird cannot be an eagle because it's eating a mouse. The information tells you hawks and eagles eat small mammals.

The other options are incorrect by a process of elimination.

11 The dog trainer claims dogs should not be fed their food from a bowl. The statement that feeding away from the bowl promotes mental and physical enrichment for the dog gives a reason to support the trainer's claim.

A is incorrect. This statement gives a reason to play games with your dog but does not give a reason to avoid feeding the dog from a bowl. Therefore it does not best support the trainer's claim.

B is incorrect. This statement is not relevant to the trainer's claim.

C is incorrect. This statement does not give a reason to avoid feeding the dog from a bowl.

12 If A were folded to make a dice and placed so that the circle was on top and the square was visible, the octagon would be to the left of the square, not to the right. All other nets are possible.

13 Compare each of the five shapes in the question diagram to the shapes in the options to work out which is exactly the same.

14 It is not a possible view after one move (or two cards flipped). The only card that has been turned over is the king (the jack was already face down). Two cards need to be turned over.

15 Liora is correct since there might be an emergency but the 'abandon ship' signal has not yet been sounded or there might be an emergency that does not require an 'abandon ship' signal. James is correct because we know the 'abandon ship' drills always happen at 3 o'clock in the afternoon. So if the signal sounds in the middle of the night, it must be a real signal and not a drill.

The other options are incorrect by a process of elimination.

NOTES